KINDRED

TENDING BAR, ENTERTAINING FRIENDS, TOASTING LIFE

Spirits

DESIGNED AND EDITED BY
CAROL HARALSON
ILLUSTRATED BY
JAQUELIN LOYD

COUNCIL OAK BOOKS

© 1992 by Council Oak Books
ISBN 0-933031-43-2
Library of Congress Number 91-73721
Council Oak Books
Tulsa, Oklahoma 74120

Printed in Singapore by Palace Press

DESIGNED AND EDITED BY CAROL HARALSON
ILLUSTRATED BY JAQUELIN LOYD

Researched and written by Carol Haralson, Christine Booth,
John Foreman, and Bradley Bowen with contributions from
Karen Rambo, Pat Manhart, Jaquelin Loyd, Edwin Wade,
Frank Robinette, Deborah Adams, and unnamed kindred spirits
whose inspired hospitality has sustained us.

CONTENTS

GATHERING KINDRED SPIRITS

RAISING A GLASS OF CHEER

GATHERING
KINDRED
SPIRITS

GATHERING KINDRED SPIRITS

"The civilized and civilizing protocol of the aperitif and its democratic cohort, the cocktail, is a sublimely conceived exercise in moderation that produces abundant satisfaction."

WARREN PICOWER

 RIENDS ARRIVE. A fire is on the hearth. Or the windows are open to a summer night and the smell of cut grass. You welcome guests to an evening of champagne cocktails and chocolate desserts. Or you greet them in paint-spattered jeans with a cold jug of Sangria, and a tray of microwaved nachos.

The ways to celebrate are as many as the reasons. But, finally, the perennial reason is simply the desire to share a moment of life with fellow travelers. And when the many ways of celebrating are numbered, they too come down to one: creating a festivity, minor or grand, in which people who have things in common are inspired by the mood and the moment to share them.

When "entertaining friends" we are in fact encouraging them to entertain each other, and themselves, by providing them with a generous occasion and a convivial atmosphere, lively company, and the delights of pure creature comfort.

How to do this? One can analyze the perfect Martini, and we will. One can probe the mysteries of the cocktail shaker and the mulling spoon, acknowledging that an exquisite libation is a great earthly gift. Many a conversation has flowed more vividly, many a *bon mot* trembled in the air with more clarity and deliciousness, between relaxed guests sipping appreciatively at perfectly composed mixed spirits or steaming cups of Irish coffee. But ultimately the delights of friendship, and the proferring of thoughtful food and drink to the loyal and loving, is about personal style. It's about you, and the people with whom you share your life. Here in one source are a number of guidelines for both classic concoctions and daring departures, along with some hospitable ideas.

After that, it's your party. And, in the words of an old toast, may you have a good appetite — for life.

The Basic Materials

GLASSWARE

Glassware for drinks is an interesting exercise in the notion that form follows function; most glasses are classified not by capacity but by general shape and their shapes often relate to the nature of the concoction they are meant to hold. Some glasses protect drinks from being warmed by the hands and others encourage this. Some are constructed to promote restrained sipping and others invite deep draughts.

Few hosts possess the full range of glassware. However, if you take into account the functional aspects of shape and size, creative substitutions can be successful and attractive. Try wide-mouthed small white wine glasses for Martinis, iced tea glasses for Collins drinks, globe-shaped red wine glasses for brandy. In our era of eclectic latitude, glasses need not all match; a visual bouquet might be livelier. When adding to your glass collection, don't overlook antique stores and flea markets, which are sometimes troves of nostalgic period glassware. Here are the basics:

Rocks or Old-Fashioned: Meant for drinks over ice, rocks glasses are approximately as tall as they are wide. Capacities vary widely, but most hold four to nine ounces.

Double Old-Fashioned: A rocks glass with double capacity.

Highball: A highball glass is twice as tall as it is wide.

Collins: Collins glasses, about three times as tall as they are wide, are meant for refreshing drinks that contain greater than average amounts of mixer. They may be frosted or clear.

Pilsner: Meant for beer, pilsners vary widely in capacity and shape. Steins and large ceramic or glass mugs with oversized handles work well. The height and shape of a good beer glass accommodates the foam or "head" that some beer aficionados prefer. Accentuate the foam by pouring directly into the center of the glass. To minimize foam, tilt the glass slightly and pour down its inside surface. Since beer usually is not drunk in tiny sips, the shape of a beer glass allows liquid to glide out.

Martini: A Martini glass (also called a cocktail glass), on the other hand, is designed for small sips and has low volume capacity. Its shape disperses the perfume of the drink and allows for restrained sipping. The stem keeps warm fingers from taking the chill off the drink.

Champagne: Either saucer-shaped, with the same merits as the Martini glass, or in the deep, narrow shape called a "flute." Flutes allow champagne to keep its bubbliness longer and they are preferred for champagne cocktails. An important aspect of either glass is the stem, which maintains the drink's chill.

Snifter: Used for sipping brandy, snifters have the reverse goal of long-stemmed glasses. Their bulbous shape nestles in the hand, allowing it to slightly warm the brandy and thus release its bouquet.

Irish coffee: Meant for drinks made with hot coffee, these glasses usually have handles or holders to keep hands from the hot glass, but often are transparent for aesthetic effect.

Shot glass: A small-capacity glass in a range of shapes. Mostly used for drinks taken straight, such as tequila Mexican style and aquavit.

Wine glass: Spherical-bodied glasses are used for red wine, served at room temperature (the wider tops release the wine's bouquet), and narrower-bodied glasses are used for white wine, usually served chilled.

TOOLS AND SUPPLIES

Blender or Cuisinart: Great for drinks with pureed fruit and ice, or with cream or ice cream.

Can and bottle openers

Champagne bucket

Cocktail shaker: For blending, aerating and chilling drinks.

Corkscrews

Cutting board and knife

Ice bucket

Jigger: Double-ended, 1½ ounces on one side, 1 ounce on the other.

Long-handled bar spoon

Paper cocktail napkins

Pitchers

Strainer: For pouring out stirred-and-chilled mixtures and leaving the ice behind.

Squeezers or manual juicers

INGREDIENTS

The bar pantry: Tabasco sauce, Worcestershire sauce, grenadine, Rose's Lime Juice, Angostura bitters, olives, cocktail onions, maraschino cherries, pepper, salt, superfine sugar (which dissolves easily in cold liquids), cinnamon, nutmeg.

The juice shelf: Tomato, lemon, grapefruit, cranberry, pineapple, and grapefruit juice.

Fresh ingredients: Lemons, limes, oranges, light cream.

Mixers: Club soda (or seltzer), tonic, ginger ale, 7-Up, colas, carbonated mineral waters and bottled water such as Perrier, Calistoga, Evian, or Appolinaris.

Ice: The more the better. Keep an extra sack in your freezer.

SPIRITS

Quantities suggested refer to numbers of different brands, not to quantities of bottles. Various distillers of the same spirit often produce liquors with quite different characteristics.

Brown whiskeys: Two blended Scotch whiskeys and one single-malt, an Irish whiskey, a Canadian whiskey, two bourbons, one Tennessee sour-mash

White goods: Two vodkas, two gins, one light rum and one dark rum, one tequila, one aquavit

Aperitifs: One sweet and one dry vermouth, two or three patent aperitifs such as Byrrh, Campari, Dubonnet, or Lillet, plus sherry, white jug wine, champagne

Brandy: One cognac, one California brandy

Liqueurs: Curaçao bitter orange: Cointreau, Grand Marnier, or generic triple sec; crème de menthe; Pernod; crème de cacao. Add to these basics any of your favorites.

WINES

Red wines: Start with two red wines from the Napa Valley of California — Cabernets are a good choice. Cabernet is the varietal name, that is, the name of the variety of grape from which the wine is mostly or entirely made. Wines from the Cabernet vine are well balanced between sweetness and dryness and are medium to full-bodied. Add two French Bordeaux red table wines. The Bordeaux region of France is the world's largest area for quality wine production and two-thirds of the wine grown there is red — mostly of the grape varieties Cabernet and Merlot. "Table wines" are blends of two or more varieties of grapes and may come from anywhere in the country of origin. They are less expensive than French *Appellation Controlée* (meaning "controlled place-name") wines. These wines are labeled with the region, village, district, or individual vineyard of their origin under strict French labeling laws meant to insure the validity of the information. You may

wish to add a couple of bottles of French *Appellation Controlée* wine; these
need not be the expensive first growth (Grand Cru) wines. To these,
add a couple of modest wines of your choice — it is well worth experi-
menting with Chilean, Spanish, Portuguese, and Australian reds. Take
advantage of your wine merchant's experience as you shop for wines. A
good way to start is to have in mind the qualities you prefer (sweet or
dry, heavy or light, for example) and a particular price range, then to ask
the wineseller to suggest some wines that fit both.

White wines: Again start with Napa varietals, two Chenin Blancs,
two Sauvignon Blancs, three or four Pinot Chardonnays. Add a spicy,
fruity Gewûrtztraminer and a Riesling in their long-necked brown
bottles, an Orvieto from Umbria, a Frascati from the countryside near
Rome, a light and fruity Vouvray from the Loire valley. And, of course,
champagne.

Bottled at the vineyard.

MIS EN BOUTEILLE AU CHATEAU

CHATEAU
LES ORMES DE PEZ

SAINT-ESTÈPHE
1987

12,5% Vol   75cml

APPELLATION SAINT-ESTEPHE CONTROLÉE

J.A.CAZES, PROPRIETAIRE A SAINT-ESTEPHE, (FRANCE)

PRODUCE OF FRANCE

Name of the vineyard.

Region in France
Vintage, year
grapes were harvested.
Appellation
d'origine Controlée
(A.O.C.),
government
regulation.

The Occasion

Although we tend to think of festivities in visual terms — color, space and movement — it is good to remember that your guests will experience a convivial occasion with all their senses. "Setting the stage" for a gathering may mean lighting candles or switching on a well-chosen tape or compact disk. It may mean opening the kitchen door so the savory smell of the dinner roast can waft through the house. One host we know always burns a nugget of piñon incense shortly before guests arrive. Anything that heightens your guests' comfort, sense of well-being, and sensory enjoyment adds to the occasion. And everything that increases your own feeling of preparedness and confidence helps you to achieve that state of pleasantly vigilant relaxation that is the hallmark of a good host. Below are a few favorite tips.

~Light from a variety of low-wattage sources adds to the feeling of spaciousness as well as mystery. Light candles, table lamps, wall sconces, avoiding bright overhead lights if possible.

~If you are serving a meal, set the table well before guests arrive, even the night before. Place candles with matches nearby.

~If you are setting an hors d'oeuvre or buffet table, choose and assemble the necessary servingware — bowls, serving spoons, trays — the day before the party and arrange them in the serving space. It will be quicker and easier to fill them just before guests arrive. Some elements of the table, such as condiments, garnishes, sauces, or cold salads, can be put in their serving bowls, covered with plastic wrap, and refrigerated hours before the party — or even the night before. Whisk them out at the last minute.

~If you are serving cheeses, remember to remove them from the refrigerator an hour or two before serving so they can come to room temperature. The same is true for butter.

~Many cocktail snacks can be made ahead. Don't choose more than one or two that require your attention at the last minute.

~If you are providing guests with fresh drinks yourself, ask a friend to be your assistant throughout the evening. Or set out the bar and invite guests to refresh their own drinks.

~Try preparing a single beverage in advance and serving it from decorative pitchers all evening. The fruity fortified red wine called Sangria works well, especially with Spanish foods. Use a glass pitcher to showcase the beautiful sliced fruit. Or try pitchers of Mimosas (champagne and orange juice) and Bloody Marys for brunch, or Margaritas for after-work drinks. Don't put ice in the pitcher — it will dilute the drink. Keep an extra pitcherful in the refrigerator.

Finally, a rewarding gathering, like a classical cocktail, depends on the proportions and chemistry of its composition — your guests. The best you can hope for is that magical evening when your friends fall in love all over again, with the moment, with life, with each other, even with themselves and their dreams. The worst that can happen is that everyone has some refreshment and goes home. And that's not so bad. So mix well, then relax.

Mixing the Perfect Drink

S pirits are mixed because aeration improves their flavor. However, the shimmer of clear drinks can be clouded by too vigorous mixing and so they are often simply stirred gently, not shaken.

An ice-filled cocktail shaker or other container is used to chill and combine drinks such as Martinis that are served cold and straight up, that is, without ice. In our times, many mixed drinks are served over ice, but the genuine classical cocktail, which became a colorful part of American social life in the 1920s, was served straight up. However, it was first shaken or stirred to a scintillating chill over hard-frozen ice. Prior to this revolution in style, drinks were often taken in the old-fashioned British way — without ice, simply poured from a handsome decanter and perhaps spritzed with a bit of seltzer. An electric blender is a boon to drinks based on fruit juices and especially to those made with thick syrups, cream, milk, or eggs.

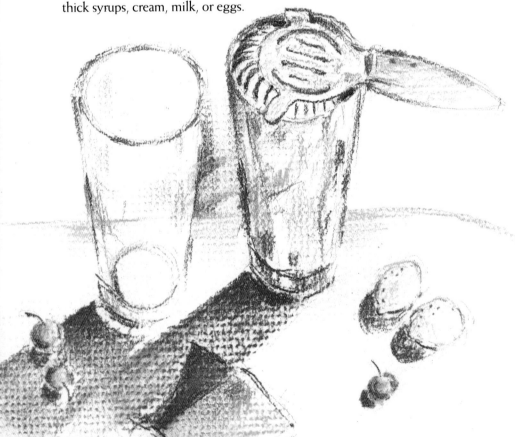

ICE: THE BIG CHILL

The sound of ice against glass is a delicate little music, a soothing signal to sit back and enjoy. Give ice its due. Fill glasses abundantly with clean, hard-frozen ice before adding chilled liquids. Contact with liquor will begin to melt the ice and you want to avoid the unfortunate look of a tall, watery drink with two or three misshapen, half-melted cubes bobbing at the top. If you have freezer space, pre-chill your cocktail glasses: rinse glasses with cold water and place them in the freezer while still wet. Chill for a minimum of half an hour. If you want sugar or salt on the rims, dip glasses before freezing.

Spirits are chilled and blended at the same time by shaking them in an ice-filled cocktail shaker or stirring them with a long-handled spoon in an ice-filled pitcher or crock. When chilling drinks this way, use clean, hard-frozen ice so that it will not overdilute the mixture you are chilling. Exact procedures are suggested with each drink recipe.

Some liquors, notably top-quality vodka and Dutch gin, take kindly to a polar atmosphere. Keep them in the freezer, where they will become syrupy but will not freeze. Many people find them delicious served simply in shot glasses in this intensely chilled state, with just a twist of citrus. For mixed cocktails, pour directly from the frozen bottles.

Ice Tips:

~Aromatic frozen foods stored in your freezer can scent your ice. If possible, keep ice in a separate compartment or seal it tightly in plastic bags.

~Keep ice fresh and cold. Always toss the old ice and start fresh before mixing another drink, ideally in a fresh, frosted glass. Also keep an eye on the quality of ice if you are using an ice bucket. Melting, "warm" ice is unappealing and quickly dilutes a drink.

~Use your imagination to create wonderful ices (see page 25 for ice-making ideas), but don't use carbonated beverages. As they melt they dilute drinks with a flat, stale taste.

~The Party Ice Rule of Thumb: Buy or make twice as much ice as you think you'll need. You'll need it.

MIXERS, GARNISHES, AND FLAVORINGS

Good cooks will warn you away from cooking with inferior wine. As in cooking, the quality of ingredients invested in cocktails does affect the result. Use the juiciest citrus, the best-quality garnishes, the freshest tonics and seltzers you can obtain. And of course, supply the best spirits your budget allows — remembering that in cocktails focusing on a single element (Martinis, for example), this matters more than in coolers or multi-ingredient drinks.

~Squeeze your own fruit juice — it adds an extraordinary deliciousness to fruit-based drinks such as Screwdrivers and Old Fashioneds.

~To make lemon and lime twists, use a small sharp knife to scrape away a swath of the yellow or green outer peel. Turn the peel over on a wooden cutting board outer-side down and remove any bitter white pith that may cling to it. Slice very thinly. Shape each strip by twisting one end clockwise and the other counter-clockwise simultaneously.

~To test the carbonation of soda water or tonic, splash a little into the kitchen sink and watch for fizz. Flat mixers make flat drinks. Carbonated mixers in ten-ounce bottles retain carbonation longer (and, of course, are used more quickly.)

~Add ingredients that can be overdone (bitters or sugar, for example) to your drink first. If you overdo it, they can be tossed out without wasting anything else.

~Add sugar first and stir until it is dissolved in the first liquid added. Bartenders often use powdered sugar, superfine sugar or sugar syrup because they dissolve more quickly than regular granulated sugar.

~Buy nutmeg whole (pecan-sized rough brown "nuts") and acquire a little nutmeg grater from a gourmet shop. The difference between freshly grated nutmeg and the preground substitute will be apparent.

SUGARS AND SYRUPS

Sucrose- or fructose-based mixtures are often used to sweeten and add flavor to sweet drinks. Examples called for in the recipes in this book are grenadine (made with pomegranate juice), orgeat syrup (which is intensely almond flavored), and Rose's Lime Juice. Professional bartenders often make their own sugar syrup to have on hand — it is made simply by adding sugar to boiling water and stirring until the sugar is dissolved. Unlike granulated sugar, such a syrup will blend completely with other liquids and will remain suspended in the berverage indefinitely (granulated sugar crystals may often end up gathered into a sweet grit at the bottom of a glass.

You can make your own sugar syrups, adding favorite herbs, spices and fruits. The two recipes below for lemon-, lime- and mint-flavored sugar syrups are versatile favorites.

~**Sugar Syrup**: *2 cups granulated sugar, 1 ¾ cups spring water.* Blend ingredients in a saucepan over medium heat, stirring until sugar is dissolved, about five minutes. Cool to room temperature and pour into a clean glass bottle. Cap and refrigerate.

~**Mint Syrup**: *2 cups sugar, 2 cups spring water, ½ cup chopped fresh mint leaves and stems, packed.* Stir sugar and water in saucepan over medium heat until sugar dissolves. Add mint, cover and simmer over low heat for 10 minutes. Let mixture cool to room temperature, pour into bottle and cap. Let syrup stand for eight hours before refrigerating.

~**Lemon or Lime Syrup**: *1 cup sugar, 1 cup spring water, 1 cup fresh lime or lemon juice.* Heat all ingredients to boiling, stirring frequently. Cover and simmer over very low heat for five minutes. Cool to room temperature, pour into bottle and cap. Let stand for eight hours before refrigerating.

~**Vanilla Sugar**: For a subtle touch of sweet vanilla, place a three-inch piece of whole vanilla bean in a pint jar filled with superfine sugar. Cover tightly and shake. Allow to stand at room temperature for at least two weeks. For a continuous supply, add more sugar to the jar as it is used. Use in coffee and other sweetened drinks when a hint of vanilla would make a delicious addition.

THE METHOD: A FEW STANDARDS

THE PERFECT MARTINI

~Use the very best gin and vermouth you can afford — it will make a difference. Imported vermouth and London Dry gin are best. There is much debate about the proper proportions of gin to vermouth. True aficionados seem to prefer a proportion of 7:1, or, if the gin is particularly superb and one wants to taste it fully, 8:1.

~Serve martinis in stemmed glasses — frosted first in the freezer. Holding the glass by the stem keeps the warmth of your fingers from taking the chill off the Martini.

~The garnish may be an olive, a twist of lemon zest, or a cocktail onion, depending on preference. If using a twist of lemon, be sure to use the yellow outer rind only as the white pith is bitter.

~Place dry, hard-frozen ice, and plenty of it, in a mixing container, either a shaker or a jug. Add the vermouth and gin. Stir with a long-handled spoon (if you are using a jug) or close the shaker top and shake for one minute. Strain immediately into chilled glasses.

~Start with fresh ice each time you prepare a drink. If you can't, be sure to strain out all liquid before adding new ingredients.

MEET THE COLLINS FAMILY

~Learn to make a Collins and you will instantly know a whole family of drinks. The basic ingredients are sweetened citrus juice and 2 ounces of liquor plus soda, but the drink varies greatly with the chosen spirit: rum, whiskey, gin, vodka, brandy, or tequila. For a Tom Collins, place the juice of half a lemon (about one ounce) and one teaspoon sugar or sugar syrup in a cocktail shaker and blend. Add ice and 2 ounces gin and shake briskly. Strain into an ice-filled Collins glass (which takes its name from this traditional drink) and top with fresh soda.

~With grapefruit juice instead of lemon juice, a Collins becomes a Salty Dog. Serve in a frozen glass with a salted rim.

~With vodka instead of gin, a Collins becomes a Greyhound — also called a Vodka Collins. In drinkmaking, as in other pursuits, nomenclature changes over time. Once a Tom Collins was always made with gin, but with the increasing popularity of vodka, a Tom Collins and a Vodka Collins are, for some, interchangeable.

~ Try orange, lemon, lime, tangerine, or grapefruit juice combined with various liquors to make your own Collins inventions.

~For Collins drinks, always used freshly squeezed citrus, not juice made from concentrate. Squeeze fruit separately for each drink. The tastiest juice has never been stored in a container other than the lovely peel and pulp of fresh fruit. While this may sound like extra trouble, a bartending friend observes that drinks made with obvious care tend to be relished with equal care, and at a stately and appreciative pace.

~One teaspoon of sugar or syrup for each Collins drink is a guideline, not a rule. You may prefer sweeter or drier drinks, or may wish to adjust the amount of sweetener according to the tartness of the fruit.

~Newly available blood oranges have deep crimson flesh and produce fruit juice that is equally vivid in color. They make beautiful Collins drinks.

~A tall, 12-ounce Collins glasses is a natural canvas for inventive garnishes. Try a spiral of zest made from the fruit you have squeezed for the drink, sprigs of mint, berries, or pretty straws and wedges of fruit.

IRRESISTABLE ALEXANDERS

~The Brandy Alexander is perhaps the best known cream drink. The traditional recipe calls for 1½ ounces brandy, 1 ounce white crème de cacao, and 1 ounce cream or milk, shaken briskly together in a cocktail shaker, strained into a cocktail glass, and garnished with freshly grated nutmeg. Vary the richness and texture by choosing heavy whipping cream, half-and-half, or milk.

~If a blender or Cuisinart is handy, the sky's the limit for blended cream drinks. Instead of milk or cream, use rich premium-grade ice cream in the flavor of your choice, from honey vanilla to Swiss mocha almond. For each drink, place a scoop of ice cream in the blender along with the spirits. Serve these thick, velvety drinks without ice.

~Flavor combinations for Alexander-style drinks are almost endless. Try brandy and crème de cocoa with peppermint stick ice cream, rum and banana liqueur with coffee ice cream, whiskey and cherry-flavored liqueur with honey vanilla ice cream, white crème de menthe and crème de chocolat with rich premium vanilla ice cream.

~Serve frozen cream drinks immediately from the blender, while the texture is still dense and thick.

~Garnish with shaved chocolate, a strawberry fan, fresh mint leaves, a sprinkling of cinnamon, freshly grated nutmeg, broken peppermint sticks. Choose a garnish that extends or complements the flavors of the drink.

~Ice cream drinks inspired by the Brandy Alexander make great desserts. Serve in saucer-shaped glasses or goblets along with chocolate cookie wafers or crunchy butter cookies.

~Toasted nuts provide an interesting texture contrast for ice cream or cream drinks. Try a topping of toasted slivered almonds or chopped walnuts.

~Try a tropical Rum Alexander made with pineapple sorbet and topped with fresh toasted coconut.

~How about a Chocolate Sundae Alexander? Top a Brandy Alexander or a variation on this delicious theme with a ribbon of melted chocolate, a maraschino cherry, and a scatttering of coarsely broken toasted pecans.

Bloody Mary "Swizzles"
Leafy celery stalks
Cucumber spears
Cinnamon sticks
Carrots
Chopsticks stuck with
 radish roses
Zucchini spears
Fresh jicama

BEST BLOODY MARYS

~Marinate lime wedges in Worcestershire sauce for a few hours before using in Bloody Marys.

~If you substitute a tablespoon of tomato paste for a like amount of tomato juice in a Bloody Mary, your drink will stay refreshingly undiluted until the last drop. This is especially useful in making up large batches for a brunch party.

~Bloody Marys are very amenable to the personal touch. Experiment with various ingredients to create your own special version. For starters, try orange juice, Clamato or clam juice, celery salt, dill seed, V-8 juice, Snappy Tom, or barbeque sauce.

~ If you don't know your guests' preferences, however, go easy on the hot sauce. You can always give your friends the Tabasco bottle so that they can intensify their drinks to taste.

~Try using a flavored vodka, such as serrano pepper or peppercorn, to give zip to the traditional Bloody Mary. See page 35 for recipes for homemade flavored vodkas.

THE SUPERB
CHAMPAGNE COCKTAIL

~True champagne can be made only in a region of the same name about 90 miles east of Paris. Other sparkling wines, however — though not, strictly speaking, champagnes — are made throughout the world. The best are made with the champagne method of individual bottle fermentation. For Champagne Cocktails choose less noble champagne or good dry sparkling wine. Save first-rate, costly, genuine champagnes for a moment when their virtues can be appreciated unadorned.

~Champagne and sparkling wines derive their relative sweetness from sugar syrup introduced into the bottles just before final corking. Driest is Brut, next driest is Extra Dry, and sweetest is Demi-Sec (with 3 to 6 percent sugar.) Choose Brut or Extra Dry for Champagne Cocktails, as you will be introducing sweetness with the sugar and bitters.

~When uncorking effervescent wines, do not to allow an explosion of foam, which releases carbonation and reduces the sparkle of the wine.

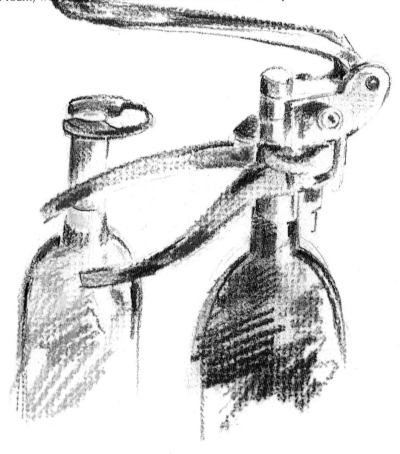

Remove the wire and metal capping material, then hold tightly to the cork as you gently rotate the bottle. If the cork does not budge, use your thumbs to slowly pry it out. Point the bottle toward the ceiling!

~Use tulip glasses or flutes, not saucer-shaped glasses, for effervescent wines. Saucer-shaped glasses dissipate the carbonation too quickly. A tulip glass is perfect for a Champagne Cocktail, as the bubbles rise gracefully from the V-shaped bottom of the glass, very slowly dispersing the sugar and bitters into the drink.

~After placing the sugar cube with bitters in the bottom of the champagne flute, pour the sparkling wine gently down the side of the glass so as to retain as much as possible of its bubbly carbonation.

FLOURISHES

One of the pleasures of entertaining friends is the excuse for momentary extravagance. Add an extra fillip with the following suggestions.

~Garnished ice. Try freezing herbs, fruits, vegetables and flowers into ice cubes. Simply drop an embellishment into each section of an ice tray, fill with spring water, and freeze. For most drinks, try lemon, lime or orange twists. For sweet or fruit-based drinks, freeze raspberries or other berries, or a pineapple chunk into each ice cube. For spicy drinks, try green or black olives, thin strips of red or green pepper, chili peppers, cocktail onions or tiny carrot curls. For savory drinks, add fresh herbs to spring water (or freeze the herbs in tomato juice). And for sheer elegance, use colorful little edible flowers — they are stunning frozen into sparkling ice cubes and floated in clear drinks.

~Chill drinks containing fruit juice with cubes of frozen juice studded with fruit. Add berries or chunks of fruit to orange or pineapple juice cubes. Make several traysful at a time and store in plastic bags.

~Cool drinks with bite-site frozen slices pineapple, peaches, kiwi, melons, or whole strawberries. Dip fruit in lemon juice, place on a large baking sheet, and freeze. When frozen solid, store in plastic bags.

~Make lemon or lime ice by mixing one-third cup lemon or lime syrup (page 19) with two cups of water. Freeze into cubes.

Great Bar Food

In some cultures, a drink is never offered without at least a little nibble of food. We think that is a fine idea. You can serve something so simple as a dish of spiced nuts, cracked olives with herbs, or crunchy sourdough bread with sharp cheddar cheese. Whatever you decide to serve in the way of food, offer it with verve and abundance.

CLASSICS

BREAD AND CHEESE

The classic of classics, bread and cheese, spans continents and generations. To please many tastes, set forth a platter of the best deli cheeses available to you: noble, blue-veined Stilton, rich triple crème (more like heavenly butter than cheese), sharp white cheddar. Add a basket of French baguettes, heated to make their crusts crunchy, then roughly cut into chunks or slices. Or serve a wheel of Brie, decorated with black, white, and green peppercorns and fresh or dried herbs, with water crackers. Experiment. Try dense, raisin-studded Pumpernickel with triple crème, toasted olive sourdough with Cheddar, but remember that cheeses with delicate, mild flavors should not be overwhelmed by spicy commercial crackers.

OLD-FASHIONED GOOD-TASTING
CHOPPED CHICKEN LIVERS

3 pounds chicken livers
5 large eggs, hard cooked
3 medium onions
neutral oil (peanut, corn, or vegetable) for sauteing
salt and freshly ground black pepper.

Trim and carefully clean the livers of all fat, strings, extraneous tissue. Separate the liver lobes so they will cook evenly. Chop one onion into rough dice. Heat a saute pan and pour in about two table-spoons of oil. Saute about one-third of the livers together with about one-third of the chopped onion. Keep the heat at medium to avoid making the livers crusty. When the livers are thoroughly cooked, remove them to a bowl. Saute half the remaining livers with the remaining chopped onion. Saute remaining livers. (Livers are sauted in batches of approximately one pound to allow them to cook evenly.) Let the livers cool to room temperature. If they are chopped while still warm, the resulting texture will be too pasty.

Cut the hard-cooked eggs into quarters and the two remaining onions into eighths. Put the eggs, onions, and livers into a food proces-sor fitted with the steel blade, and process for two or three seconds. If a processor or blender is unavailable, hand-dice the ingredients as finely and evenly as possible. Taste. Add salt, if necessary, and pepper. If the mixture is too dry to be spreadable, cut in some bits of butter and mix them around with a fork. Refrigerate. Serve with rye bread, toasted pita triangles, or crackers of any kind.

COCKTAIL SANDWICHES

Guests love to make their own miniature cocktail sandwiches. The day before the party, roast a turkey breast and a small dry-cured ham. Before guests arrive, slice meats paper-thin and heap them in generous mounds on a tray. Serve with a basketful of potato rolls, egg rolls or other soft, flavorful little silver-dollar sized breads, plus a selection of spreads (mayonnaise with capers and fresh dill, grainy Dijon mustard blended with a little softened butter, commercially prepared sweet-hot mustard, horseradish and cream, or other favorites).

FRUITS OF THE SEASON

VODKA MELON BOAT

⅔ 750 ml bottle vodka

1 small can frozen lime juice concentrate, thawed

½ cup superfine sugar, or to taste

1 watermelon

1 cantaloupe

1 honeydew melon

1 quart strawberries

1 pint blueberries

2 cups fresh pineapple chunks

In a large glass pitcher, stir together vodka, lime juice and sugar until sugar is well dissolved. Set aside. Carefully slice the lengthwise top one-third from the watermelon. Use a melon baller to scoop out the fruit, placing it in a very large glass bowl. Pour any juice left in the watermelon shell into bowl with the fruit. Form a decorative edge by cutting two-inch points around the shell. Use paper towels to pat dry the inside walls, then place shell in freezer. Form melon balls from the cantaloupe and honeydew and add to the watermelon balls. Add strawberries, blueberries and pineapple. Pour vodka mixture over and carefully mix fruit. Cover with plastic wrap and refrigerate one to three hours, gently stirring once or twice an hour. To serve, nestle frozen watermelon shell into a deep tray of crushed ice. Pour a heaping portion of marinated fruit into shell. Refrigerate remaining fruit and use later to replenish the shell.

MINTED PINEAPPLE SPEARS

A quantity of fresh pineapples

Fresh Bing or sour cherries

12- inch bamboo skewers

Fresh mint leaves

Cut pineapple into bite-sized chunks and spear several chunks on each skewer, alternating occasionally with a pitted cherry, or other favorite fruit. Sprinkle a trayful of skewered fruit with coarsely chopped fresh mint leaves. Optional: You may opt to presoak the fruit in sweetened spirits of your choice, for example Kirsch, brandy, and honey for the cherries.

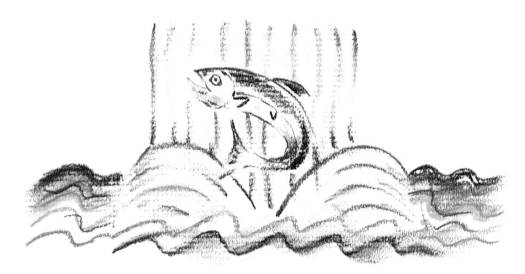

LITTLE GLORIES

POACHED SALMON

For a spectacular effect, poach a whole four- to five-pound salmon, which can be done without a great deal of trouble, even if you don't own a fish poacher. Wrap the fish in aluminum foil (oiled, so the fish won't stick to it) with 6 scallions, some salt, black pepper, the juice of half a lemon. Put the wrapped-up fish on a cookie sheet and bake it for about 40 minutes in a 425°F oven. Pierce the flesh with a fork to see if it's done. If it doesn't separate easily into moist flakes, cook it a little longer, then check again. Remove from the oven, cool, then store in your refrigerator inside the foil. Serve with good toasted bread.

COCKTAIL SHRIMP

Shrimp is great party fare and is easy to cook. Drop three pounds of large shelled and deveined shrimp into a deep kettle of boiling salted water. Cook until the shrimp are pink, about four minutes. Or, for variety, cook them in beer spiced with a bit of dry mustard, freshly-ground black pepper, and several dashes of Tabasco. Leave the tails on so your guests can get a grip on them, or provide cocktail picks or toothpicks. Serve with store-bought cocktail sauce—or make it yourself. Decorate the platter with washed but uncut blades of celery, with their frilly green tops, also good dipped in cocktail sauce.

Marinated Shrimp

Spicy marinated shrimp can be made the day before you serve them. Wash, peel and devein approximately two pounds shrimp, leaving the tails intact if you wish. Pour ½ cup olive oil into a large skillet. Toss in one to two thinly sliced white or purple onions and saute. Add the herbs of your choice: springs of tarragon, dried crumbled thyme, rosemary, bay leaves, fresh marjoram, Cajun seasonings, cumin seed, whole cloves, whole peppercorns. For spicy shrimp, add two to three crumbled dried hot red chile peppers or fresh or pickled jalapeños. Add cracked black pepper, salt, and a pinch of sugar. When the saute is aromatic and onions are transparent, add ½ cup good wine vinegar. Return to full heat. Add the shrimp and cook over medium heat four to five minutes, until shrimp are pink and beginning to curl slightly. Remove from heat, cool, cover, and refrigerate overnight or for several hours. Serve with crusty sourdough bread. Delicious with frozen vodka.

GINGERED SHRIMP

⅔ cup vegetable oil
grated peel and juice of one small lemon
¼ cup plus 2 tablespoons soy sauce
1 garlic clove, crushed
1 teaspoon finely grated ginger root
½ teaspoon dried marjoram, or 1 teaspoon fresh
1½ pounds fresh jumbo shrimp, peeled and deveined
bacon strips, plus sprigs of marjoram and lemon twists for garnish

Whisk together first six ingredients to make a marinade. Turn shrimp in marinade. Refrigerate two hours, basting occasionally. Wrap each shrimp with a bacon strip. Thread shrimp onto wooden skewers and cook over hot coals 7-10 minutes, turning frequently. Shrimp will be opaque when done. Garnish and serve with Sesame Soy Dip.

To make Sesame Soy Dip: Whisk together ½ cup light soy sauce, 4 tablespoons dark sesame oil, 4 tablespoons rice (or white) vinegar, 1 clove minced garlic, a dash of hot red pepper and 2 chopped green onions.

PARMESAN CHICKEN WINGS

1½ pounds chicken wings, cut in half at the joint
¼ cup melted butter
1 cup freshly grated Parmesan cheese
¼ teaspoon each dried marjoram and thyme
½ teaspoon dried oregano
1 teaspoon seasoned salt
2 cups bread crumbs
cracked black pepper

Mix together the cheese, spices, and bread crumbs. Dip wings into melted butter and then into crumb mixture. Place on a baking sheet and bake 30-35 minutes in a preheated oven at 350°, turning once to brown evenly. *Note: You can prepare the chicken wings up to a week ahead and freeze them. Remove them from the freezer the day of the party and pop them into the oven just before serving.*

CCRRUNCH!

POPPYSEED BREADSTICKS

3 cups all purpose flour

1½ teaspoons salt

1½ cups water, or as needed

2 teaspoons sugar

2 teaspoons active dry yeast

2 tablespoons black poppyseed

2 egg yolks whisked with ½ cup milk

Combine the flour and salt in a food processor and let the machine run as you gradually add the water, sugar, and yeast. Process until the dough forms a mass, adding a little more water if necessary. Turn the dough out onto a floured board and knead 4-5 minutes. Cover with plastic wrap and refrigerate for 1 hour. Roll out the dough into ¼-inch-thick sheets, working with a small portion at a time and using as few strokes as possible. Dust with flour as needed to prevent sticking. Let the rolled-out dough rest about 10 minutes, then cut it into ¾-inch strips. Preheat oven to 375°. Cut strips in 8-inch lengths and place on buttered baking sheets. Brush with egg mixture and sprinkle with poppyseeds. Bake until golden, about 12-14 minutes. Cool on wire racks and store at room temperature. *Note: Vary breadsticks by sprinkling some with sesame seeds, fennel seeds, hot red pepper flakes, and/or coarsely cracked salt.*

BENNE WAFERS

1 cup flour mixed with ¼ teapsoon Coleman's Dry Mustard, ¼ teaspoon salt, and ¼ teaspoon cayenne

2 cups grated Cheddar cheese blended with ¼ teaspoon Worcestershire sauce and ½ cup butter (one stick) at room temperature

¼ cup white sesame seeds plus ¼ cup black sesame seeds

Toast the sesame seeds at 350° for 15 minutes and set aside. Blend the butter and cheese. Gradually add the flour mixture, then incorporate the sesame seeds. Roll into walnut-sized balls and place on an unbuttered baking sheet. Flatten each slightly with a fork. Bake at 350° for 12-15 minutes until golden but not too brown. Wafers keep well for several days in an airtight container. *Note: Spicy Benne Wafers are great with jalapeño pepper jelly and cream cheese. Serve them with strongly flavored drinks or beer.*

PERENNIAL FAVORITE

PIZZA-IN-A-PAN

1 cup semolina flour

⅓ cup hot water

1 teaspoon baking powder

½ teaspoon salt

1 tablespoon extra virgin olive oil

Grated cheese: Jarlsberg or Mozzarella

Herbs/Seasonings: Your choice of fresh or dried marjoram, basil, oregano, thyme, rosemary plus cracked black pepper and salt

Toppings: Your choice: cooked Italian hot sausage; pepperoni; marinated artichoke hearts; sauted garlic, green onions, yellow squash, and zucchini; pine nuts; olives; lightly steamed asparagus; hearts of palm; roasted red bell peppers; Canadian bacon — whatever suits your taste.

Make the pizza dough in a food processor. Combine flour, water, baking powder, salt, and oil and process until the dough masses together. Cover wtih plastic wrap and let rest for at least 15 minutes or up to 2 hours. You can make this a day ahead and keep it in the refrigerator until needed. (It also freezes.) When you're ready to make pizzas, roll the dough into a log and cut it in 4 pieces. Roll out each into a 7-inch round. Cover the rounds with plastic wrap. Heat a 9- or 10-inch cast-iron or very heavy skillet over moderate heat. Place one of the dough rounds in the skillet, reduce heat to low, cover, and cook until the crust is dark brown on the bottom, about 3 minutes. Check after 2 minutes and adjust heat to avoid burning the dough. Remove the crust from the skillet and cover with cheese, toppings, and seasonings. Sprinkle with olive oil. Return the pizza to the skillet and cook at medium temperature, covered, until the cheese melts, about 2 mintues. Repeat with the other three rounds of dough. Cut into quarters and serve as hors d'oeuvres.

Tastings

tasting features variations on a single theme —
creating abundant opportunity for discrimination,
discussion, and a range of delightful sensations.

A VODKA TASTING PARTY

Europeans have been flavoring spirits at least since the 5th century,
when Greeks and Romans flavored wine with all manner of botanicals.
Flavoring vodka has been a time-honored tradition in eastern Europe
since the drink was invented in the 14th century. Peter the Great
reportedly loved his *pertsovka*, made by infusing vodka with black-and-
white peppercorns. The Poles are partial to the aromatic and slightly
bitter taste of *zubrovka*, vodka steeped with buffalo grass. Brandy- and
honey-laced *Yubileyneya osobaya*, or jubilee vodka, was drunk on special
occasions, as was *starka*, vodka steeped in apple and pear leaves and aged
in old wine casks for ten years.

At a tasting party, serve tots (short shots) in frosted small shot
glasses and be sure to keep the vodkas freezing cold. Vodka bottles may
be packed in ice sleeves. To make an ice sleeve, set a bottle of thoroughly chilled vodka in a clean half-gallon milk or ice cream carton. Fill

the carton with
very cold water,
freeze solid,
then cut
away the
paper
carton. Fold
a colorful
cloth napkin
into a triangle,
then into a three-
inch band and tie
around the ice
sleeve to make

handling easy. For visual interest, toss a few sprigs of herbs, flowers, or a long citrus peel spiral into the chilled water before freezing. If you wish, you can identify the various bottles by the decorative elements frozen into the ice sleeves.

Crusty bread and a selection of cheeses are great accompaniments for frozen vodka.

MAKING FLAVORED VODKAS

Vodka is flavored by infusing, or steeping, it with spices, herbs, vegetables or fruits. There are three important rules of thumb:

~Always start with premium grade vodka.

~Selecting flavoring ingredients that are fresh and ripe but not overripe.

~Milder flavors may take more time to fully infuse. The recipes that follow usually call for 24 to 48 hours of steeping, but some ingredients such as sweet fruits may take longer. On the other hand, strong flavors can quickly become overpowering. Sample flavors such as lemon peel, peppers, cumin after 24 hours.

~Flavoring favorites you may want to try in addition to the following recipes include: Apples, bitter orange, black currants, blueberries, cranberries, grapefruits, plums, pineapple, raspberries, tangerines and black cherries and peaches with their cracked pits, absinthe substitutes, black tea, caraway, cardamom, cinnamon, cocoa, coffee beans, coriander, cumin, dill, fennel, juniper, mint, rosemary, sage and thyme, almonds and hazelnuts, rose petals and violets.

~When you find an infused vodka you really like, think about making a batch of it for gifts — perfect for party or housewarming presents. Decorative bottles are available in kitchenware shops, or you can recycle empty liquor bottles by soaking off the labels.

For mini-bottles, use one-third the amount of spice called for in the following recipes.

~**Clove Vodka:** 1 liter premium vodka, 20 whole cloves. Add cloves to vodka and infuse at room temperature for 24 hours, turning bottle several times. Taste. Infuse up to 48 hours. Strain into clean bottle, cap and freeze.

~**Vanilla Vodka:** 1 liter premium vodka, 2 large vanilla bean pods. Add vanilla beans to vodka and infuse at room temperature for 24 hours, turning bottle several times. Taste. Infuse up to 48 hours. Strain into clean bottle, cap and freeze.

~**Citrus Vodka (Limonovka):** 1 liter premium vodka, 1 orange, lemon or lime. Use vegetable peeler to remove zest in one strip, being careful to avoid the bitter white portion of the rind. Add peel to vodka, infuse 24 to 48 hours, turning bottle several times. Strain into clean bottle and freeze.

~**Pepper Vodka:** 1 liter premium vodka, 1 hot red chile pepper. Place pepper in vodka and let steep for 24 hours, turning bottle several times. Taste. Let infuse longer, if desired, sampling every six hours. Strain into a clean bottle, cap and freeze.

~**Apricot Vodka:** 1 liter premium vodka, 1 dozen dried apricots, 6 diced apricot pits (optional). Place apricots and pits in vodka and steep 48 hours or longer, turning bottle several times daily. Strain into a clean bottle, cap and freeze. Pits add a more intense, bitter flavor.

~**Lemon-Pepper Vodka:** 1 liter vodka, 4 dozen mixed black and white peppercorns, peel of 1 lemon. Peel zest from lemon and put it and peppercorns into vodka for 48 hours, turning bottle several times daily. Strain into a clean bottle, cap and freeze.

~**Fruit Vodka Liqueur:** 1 liter premium vodka, 2 cups sugar, 1 pound fresh fruit (raspberries, strawberries, etc.). Place all ingredients in a large glass container, cover tightly and store in cool, dark place, shaking container every two days to mix the flavors. After two months, strain into a clean bottle and cap.

See page 130 for recipes using flavored vodkas.

A MAKE-IT-YOURSELF COFFEE BAR

Present guests with rich, aromatic coffee, a trayful of jewel-colored bottled liqueurs, a selection of flavored whipped creams and garnishes — and let them make their own delicious dessert coffee drinks. This treat can follow a formal dinner or a backyard barbecue, or be a party on its own.

The week before the party, begin making coffee ice cubes and storing them in plastic bags in the freezer.

The morning of the party, prepare a selection of flavored whipped creams. Whip a quantity of heavy whipping cream manually with a whisk or in an electric mixer. Apportion the cream into several small serving bowls. Then add different flavors to each one: a little sugar and brandy; kirsch; vanilla liqueur; Cointreau and grated orange zest; or any flavors you prefer. Cover with plastic wrap and refrigerate. See page 84 for a whipped cream recipes.

Just before presenting the coffee bar to friends, make the best and freshest pots of regular and decaffeinated coffee you can brew. (See pages 80-83). Set out liqueurs and whiskeys, flavored creams and plain cream, pots of coffee, garnishes and spices, and coffee ice cubes for cold drinks, along with mugs and Irish Coffee glasses, spoons, and, if you like, little tent cards with handwritten coffee drink recipes.

Some ideas for the coffee buffet:

Coffee and espresso

Cream: Flavored whipped creams (see page 84), plain cream, half-and-half

Sugar: Plain white sugar, vanilla sugar (page 21), brown sugar

Liqueurs and whiskeys: Amaretto, Anisette, apricot brandy, Bailey's Irish Cream, bourbon, brandy, Chambord, chocolate mint liqueur, Cointreau, crème de banana, crème de cacao, crème de menthe, Grand Marnier, Irish whiskey, coffee-flavored liqueur, Kirsch, praline liqueur, dark and light rum, whiskeys, Tia Maria, triple sec, vodka

Garnishes: Cocoa, chocolate curls, grated chocolate, lemon and orange zest, candy canes, chocolate coffee beans, cinnamon sticks, toasted coconut, cloves, nutmeg, allspice, fresh mint sprigs

Serve crunchy double-baked Italian cookies called *biscotti* (meaning "toasted"), for dipping.

B I S C O T T I

3 cups sifted flour
1 tablespoon baking powder
¼ teaspoon salt
5 egg whites
1 cup sugar
5 egg yolks
1-3 tablespoons anise, almond, hazelnut or other liqueur

Sift dry ingredients together. Beat egg whites to soft peaks. Sprinkle sugar over whites and beat stiff. Fold in egg yolks and liqueur. Blend well. Sprinkle flour mixture over egg mixture gradually, folding well continuously. Pour batter onto two buttered baking sheets, forming 3 x 14 x ¾-inch rectangles. Bake in preheated oven at 375° about 30 minutes. Remove from oven and cool. Slice across rectangles, 1 inch thick. Place slices on their sides on unbuttered baking sheets and toast at 400° until lightly browned, about 8-10 minutes.

CHOCOLATE NUT CRESCENTS

1 cup plus 2 tablespoons flour

1 cup plus 2 tablespoons ground nuts (hazelnuts, pecans, almonds)

¾ cup unsalted butter at room temperature

½ cup sugar

1 large egg yolk

6 ounces bittersweet or semisweet chocolate, melted

2 tablespoons finely chopped nuts

Combine first 5 ingredients into a smooth dough. Pinch off 2 teaspoonsful at a time, roll up, and bend into crescent shape. Place crescents on unbuttered baking sheet and flatten slightly. Bake about 15 minutes in preheated oven at 350°. Cool on sheets 10 minutes, then move to racks. Dip half of each crescent into melted chocolate and roll in nuts.

A CHAMPAGNE EVENING

Build a magical evening around bright, bubbly champagne. Present three to five champagnes for tasting (each in an ice-filled champagne bucket) and set out a selection of liqueurs that marry well with sparkling wine, plus garnishes and flavorings. Save the finer champagnes for plain sipping and use one of less robust merit for mixing with other flavors in a series of variations on the lovely Champagne Cocktail.

To gild the lily, serve freshly cut apple slices (dip in lemon juice to prevent browing), dried apricots, banana slices, and strawberries with a fondue pot filled with chocolate (made with 8 ounces melted semisweet chocolate, a 14-ounce can of sweetened condensed milk, and ⅓ cup milk) and let guests dip fruits in chocolate. Or serve a rich chocolate torte cut in thin slices and adorned with fresh fruit.

You will need:

Champagne: For the tasting, select two or three fine French champagnes in a range of dryness and chill to perfection. For the Champagne Cocktails, select a good dry sparkling wine such as Freixenet.

Liqueurs: Crème de cassis, Chambord, armagnac, cognac or brandy, B & B.

Garnishes and flavorings: Bitters, sugar cubes, fresh mint leaves, lemon, lime and orange twists, cherries, strawberries, and black currants if available.

PORTS AND TORTES

Port, a sweet red fortified wine, is usually served after a meal. It takes its name from the town of Oporto, sited at the mouth of the Douro River in the Port-producing region of northern Portugal. In 1968, the Portuguese government attempted to distinguish true Port from imitations by declaring that Port shipped to the United States must be labeled *Porto*. However, some Portuguese shippers continue to label their bottles "Port," which is still the most common name for this drink, a traditional favorite in France and England.

At a certain point in their fermentation, the crushed grapes destined to be Port are mixed with brandy, which suddenly stops the fermentation process. Consequently Port contains both unfermented grape sugar and alcohol. The great majority of Port — called Ruby or Tawny — is aged in wooden casks, or pipes, for several years. Ruby Port is dark and fruity. Tawny Port is lighter, more delicate, often more complex in flavor. True Tawny Port has been aged longer than Ruby, but many Tawny Ports on the market have been blended with white Port to make them lighter and softer. Ruby and Tawny Ports are ready to drink when bottled and do not improve with age. The rarer and more glamorous Vintage Port, however, does improve with keeping. It is made entirely from the grapes of a single harvest and bottled after about two years in the cask, so it matures in the bottle rather than in wood. A shipper "declares" a vintage only when he thinks the quality of the wine warrants it — three or four times a decade, usually. Vintage Port needs ten or fifteen years in the bottle to be drinkable, and, once sufficiently aged, can be among the most superb and complex of wines.

Treat your guests to a late-night Port evening, either after dinner or as an event on its own. Select three or four fine Ports, including a Ruby, a Tawny, and one or two well-aged Vintage Ports. Decant the bottle-aged Vintage Ports carefully, as there tends to be sediment in the bottom of the bottles. Pour small glasses of the various Ports, so guests can compare the differences in flavors and sensations.

Along with this Porto extravaganza, offer chocolate and fruit tortes (homemade or purchased from a good bakery.) Or slice fresh pears and set them out with a wedge of Stilton, table water crackers, and shelled walnuts. Add moonlight, soft spring air if available, and the right mix of music for a splendid evening.

RAISING A GLASS OF CHEER

BOURBON, SCOTCH & OTHER WHISKIES

BOURBON

*B*ourbon is the classic American whiskey, distilled from corn. Its history is intimately associated with the early history of this country. Rum was the prevalent distilled liquor of colonial days, but early in the 18th century Scotch and Irish settlers in the eastern states began to make whiskey in pot stills. Farmers to the west who had been growing rye and barley soon discovered that it was easier and more profitable to distill their grain into whiskey than to transport the grain to market. In 1791 the new federal government, in search of sources of revenue, imposed an excise tax on whiskey. In the ensuing confrontation, riots broke out and some tax collectors were tarred and feathered. In 1794 President George Washington sent in the militia to put down the so-called Whiskey Rebellion.

To escape the long arm of the revenue collectors, some farmer-distillers pushed further west. In Kentucky they found sweet limestone-filtered spring water, ideal for making whiskey. At first their whiskey was made of rye, but eventually they exploited the abundant supply of local corn. A Baptist minister, Elijah Craig, is credited with making the first corn whiskey in Kentucky, named for Bourbon County, where it was produced. By some lucky accident it was discovered that aging the corn whiskey in charred oak barrels gave the liquor a superior flavor.

Today bourbon by law must be made from a mash of at least 51 percent corn. It is distilled in large patent, or column, stills, and is aged in new charred oak casks. Most bourbon is still made in Kentucky.

The term "sour mash," which often appears on bourbon labels, refers to the yeasting process. In the sour mash method, which is preferred for producing bourbon, fermentation is precipitated by adding the residue from a prior distillation as a portion of the new mash. This residue is called "sour" because of its acid content; the resultant whiskey is not sour at all. In the sweet mash method, which is rarely used to make U.S. whiskey, only fresh yeast is added to the new mash.

The terminology applied to American whiskeys can be confusing. *Straight bourbon*, the most prized bourbon, must be made by a single distillery during a single distilling season. It must be distilled at no higher than 160 proof and aged in wood at least two years; generally, it is aged four to six years or more. *Blended straight bourbon* is a blend of two or more straight bourbons. *Blended bourbon* is a blend containing at least 20 percent straight bourbon, with the balance consisting of flavorless neutral spirits of 190 or higher proof. The lower the proof at which whiskey is distilled, the more full-bodied and flavorful it is. The blended bourbons are lighter in taste and less expensive than the straights.

(The term "bottled in bond" which appears on some bourbon labels refers to an arrangement for postponing the payment of excise taxes while whiskey is being aged. The term is in no way to be interpreted as a guarantee of quality. Only straight whiskeys of 100 proof are bottled in bond. The whiskey is stored in a government warehouse for at least four years, and the excise tax is not paid until it is removed from the warehouse to be sold.)

SCOTCH

Steeped in tradition and lore, Scotch whisky traces its roots to the *uisge beatha*, or "water of life," invented by the ancient Celts as long ago as the 10th century. Both the Scots and the Irish lay claim to inventing whiskey, a controversy that may help explain the difference in spelling, with the Scotch (and the Canadians) omitting the "e" in whisky, and the Irish (and the Americans) retaining it.

Like all whiskeys, Scotch is distilled from a fermented mash made of grain and water, but it has a taste different from any other, with a distinctive tang of malted barley. Malting consists of soaking barley in water and then spreading it out to germinate, releasing an enzyme that converts starch to fermentable sugar. At the critical moment, germination is stopped by drying the "green malt" in a kiln over a peat fire. The peat smoke permeates the malt, imparting a characteristic smoky taste to the distilled spirit. A third distinctive component of Scotch is the highly prized water of the Scottish Highland streams, each stream contributing a unique flavor to the local whisky.

There are two types of Scotch whisky — single malt Scotches, strong-flavored and full-bodied; and the lighter, finely balanced blended Scotches. The single malts are produced from malted barley only. They are double distilled in the traditional copper pot stills, similar in shape to giant kettles, which must be emptied and recharged after each distilling cycle. Each distillery has its own process for making single malts, and the resultant whiskies are as different as French wines from different chateaux. Renowned brands of single malt Scotch include Glenlivet, Glen Grant, Talisker, Laphroaig, Glenfiddich, and Glendullen, among many others. Single malt Scotch is a connoisseur's drink, meant for sipping. It should be taken neat, on the rocks, or perhaps with a splash of spring water. Despite a recent increase in its popularity in this country, single malt Scotch constitutes only a tiny percentage of the Scotch consumed worldwide.

Blended Scotch, which most people drink, is very different from the single malt varieties. Blended Scotch is made by combining single malts with unmalted grain whiskies. The grain whiskies are produced in modern patent or column stills, whose operation is continuous so they can be emptied and charged without interrupting the distillation process. Blended whiskies are preferred for cocktails or for drinking on the rocks.

After distillation, all Scotch is aged for at least three years in oak. The casks may be new, or may be used sherry or whiskey kegs. Malt whiskies require longer aging, up to 12 to 15 years, to achieve their smooth finish; grain whiskies are best aged 6 to 8 years.

Some 98 percent of all Scotland's whisky production, both single malt and grain whisky, goes into blended whisky. A typical blended Scotch might contain some 15 to 50 different whiskies, each contributing a special flavor and aroma to the final blend. The blender's task is to recreate a uniform product, year after year, relying on his nose rather than taste to achieve the perfect marriage of ingredients; the blend is then returned to wood casks for six to nine months before its final bottling.

OTHER WHISKIES

Next to straight bourbon, blended whiskey is the most popular whiskey in America. Originally developed during World War II to extend dwindling stocks of aged Scotch and bourbon, U.S. blended whiskey by law must contain at least 20 percent straight whiskey, aged two years or more. The balance is made up of high-proof neutral grain spirits. As many as 75 different spirits might be combined in a single blended whiskey. The resulting product has a light, smooth taste, without the smokiness of Scotch or the pungency of bourbon. Blended whiskeys make excellent mixers.

The Canadian government has fewer regulations than the U.S. concerning grain type, distilling proofs, or woods used for aging, leaving the Canadian distillers a freer hand in creating their blended whiskies. Made of a mash of fermented grains, usually rye, corn, and barley, Canadian whisky is aged for a minimum of three years, and usually for six years or more. The light, delicate flavor of Canadian whisky makes it popular for sipping straight as well as mixing. Among the prominent labels are Canadian Club, Crown Royal, and Seagram's V.O. As with Scotch, Canadian whisky is spelled without the "e."

One of the first whiskeys made in the New World, rye is made in essentially the same way as bourbon, except that the mash must consist of at least 51 percent rye, which gives it a characteristic strong taste. Rye whiskey used to be more popular than it is today, and it is often confused with blended whiskey. When people order highballs such as rye and ginger or rye and soda, what they generally expect is blended whiskey; they would probably be shocked at the assertive flavor of true rye. Straight rye whiskey must be aged at least two years in new charred oak; Old Overholt is one of the few remaining premier labels.

The dispute as to whether the Irish or the Scotch invented whiskey will probably never be resolved. Irish whiskey used to be very popular in the United States until it was displaced by Scotch. Like Scotch, Irish whiskey is made from a mash based on barley, along with corn and rye. The important difference is that the malted barley is dried in smokeless coal-fired ovens rather than over peat, and so Irish whiskey lacks the smoky taste of Scotch. Straight Irish whiskeys are triple distilled in the traditional pot stills, while blended Irish whiskey combines straight whiskey with grain spirits from patent stills. Because taxes on whiskey are so high in Ireland, a great deal of illegal home brew, or *poteen*, is made in pot stills — the source of the common misconception that Irish whiskey is made from potatoes. Most Irish whiskey is aged for seven years before shipping. It has a clean, smooth, malty taste, well adapted to serving on the rocks or in mixed drinks.

Tennessee whiskey is essentially a straight bourbon, made in Tennessee from a mash that contains at least 51 percent corn, or any other grain. After distillation it is filtered through charcoal made from Tennessee maple, which gives it an outstanding mellow taste.

Sauces with Spirits

BOURBON-CARAMEL DESSERT SAUCE

1/2 cup sugar, 1/4 cup heavy cream, 2 tablespoons bourbon plus 2 tablespoons water.

Cook sugar in a heavy skillet over moderately high heat, stirring constantly with a fork. Sugar will melt and become caramel colored. Remove from heat and stir a little to cool. Pour the cream into the side of the skillet (caramel will harden as cream is added). Add bourbon and water. Return skillet to moderate heat and stir until the caramel is dissolved into the cream. Serve while still warm. Sauce will harden when fully cooled.

WHISKEY, LEMON AND CAPER SAUCE
FOR BROILED FISH

2-4 tablespoons butter, 2-4 tablespoons whiskey, 1 tablespoon capers, squeeze of fresh lemon (plus grated lemon zest if desired), dash cayenne and pinch salt, handful of coarsely chopped Italian parsley or cilantro

Start with either the roasting pan in which the fish was broiled (with fish essence still in the pan) or a clean saucepan. Melt butter and add whiskey, lemon, capers, cayenne, and salt. Cook over moderately high heat until alcohol has evaporated from whiskey and flavors are blended. Pour over broiled fish and garnish with parsley or cilantro.

BOURBON CREAM GLAZE FOR ROASTED MEAT

1/4 cup bourbon, 2 tablespoons butter, diced fresh garlic, shallots, and/or fresh herbs of choice, 1/4 to 1/2 cup cream

Start with the skillet or roasting pan in which the meat was cooked. Pour off fat but leave the crusty bits and meat essence. Add bourbon and butter to the pan and stir to mix with meat essence. Add garlic, shallots and/or herbs if desired. Simmer 5-10 minutes, then remove garlic, shallots and herbs with a slotted spoon. Cook until reduced to a glaze. Add cream and simmer until thickened slightly. Pour over roasted meat.

Scotch

THE CLASSICS

SCOTCH AND SODA

1½ ounces scotch
3 ounces very cold club soda or seltzer water

Fill a highball glass with ice, pour scotch and soda, stir.

ROB ROY

2 ounces scotch
½ ounce sweet vermouth

Combine ingredients with ice in a mixing glass, stir well, strain into a cocktail glass or over fresh ice in a rocks glass. Garnish with a lemon twist. *Note: A Dry Rob Roy is made with dry vermouth instead of sweet; a Perfect Rob Roy is made with ¼ ounce dry vermouth and ¼ ounce sweet vermouth (cf. Martinis and Manhattans).*

AFFINITY OR PERFECT ROB ROY

1 ounce scotch
1 ounce dry vermouth
1 ounce sweet vermouth
2 dashes Angostura bittes

Combine all ingredients with ice in a mixing glass. Stir well, strain into a chilled cocktail glass or over fresh ice in a rocks glass. Garnish with a twist.

RUSTY NAIL

1½ ounces scotch
1½ ounces Drambuie

Fill rocks glass with ice, add scotch and Drambuie and stir.

SCOTCH MIST

2 ounces scotch

Fill a rocks glass with crushed ice, pour scotch, add lemon twist.

BALMORAL

1½ ounces scotch
1 ounce gin
½ ounce anisette

Shake ingredients briskly with ice in a cocktail shaker, strain into a chilled cocktail glass.

BOBBY BURNS

1½ ounces scotch
½ ounce dry vermouth
½ ounce sweet vermouth
1 dash Benedictine

Combine all ingredients with ice in a mixing glass, stir evenly, strain into a cocktail glass.

CONTINENTAL

1½ ounces scotch
1 ounce coffee liqueur
1½ ounces cream or milk

Shake ingredients briskly with ice in a cocktail shaker, strain into a highball glass over fresh ice.

GODFATHER

1½ ounces scotch
1 ounce Amaretto
Pour over ice in a small rocks glass, stir.

HIGHLAND FLING

1½ ounces scotch
1 teaspoon superfine sugar
3 ounces milk

Combine ingredients with ice in a cocktail shaker, shake briskly, strain into a chilled wine glass. Garnish with grated nutmeg.

HOOTS MAN

2 ounces scotch
1 ounce Lillet
1 ounce sweet vermouth

Combine ingredients in a mixing glass with ice, stir evenly, strain over fresh ice in a chilled wine glass.

HOT SCOTCH TODDY

1½ ounce scotch
¾ cup water
1 tablespoon superfine sugar
1 slice lemon
2 whole cloves
cinnamon stick

Combine all ingredients except scotch in a small saucepan and bring to a boil over medium heat. Remove pan from heat and stir in scotch. Pour into a warmed mug.

JOE COLLINS

1½ ounces scotch
1 ounce lemon juice
1 teaspoon superfine sugar
club soda or seltzer water

In a cocktail shaker, dissolve sugar in lemon juice. Add ice, scotch and soda. Shake, strain over fresh ice in a Collins glass, top off with club soda or seltzer. *Note: Bottled sweet and sour mix may be substituted for the lemon juice and sugar.*

LOCH LOMOND

2 ounces scotch
3 dashes Angostura bitters
1 teaspoon superfine sugar

Combine ingredients with ice in a cocktail shaker. Shake briskly and strain over fresh ice.

MIAMI BEACH

1½ ounces scotch
1½ ounces dry vermouth
1 ounce grapefruit juice

Combine ingredients with ice in a mixing glass. Stir well, strain over fresh ice in a highball glass.

MICKEY WALKER

2 ounces scotch
1 ounce sweet vermouth
1 dash lemon juice
1 dash grenadine

Briskly shake ingredients with ice in a cocktail shaker, strain over ice in a rocks glass.

PURPLE HEATHER

1½ ounces scotch
½ ounce crème de cassis
club soda or seltzer water

Fill a highball glass with ice, add scotch and crème de cassis, top off with club soda or seltzer, stir lightly.

SCOTCH SIDECAR

1½ ounces scotch
1 ounce Cointreau
½ ounce lemon juice

In a cocktail shaker, combine all ingredient with ice, shake briskly and strain into a chilled cocktail glass.

SWEET PEAT

1½ ounces scotch
½ ounce cherry brandy
½ ounce sweet vermouth
½ ounce orange juice

Briskly shake all ingredients with ice in a cocktail shaker, strain into a chilled cocktail glass.

VELVET HAMMER

1½ ounces scotch
½ ounce Drambuie or crème de cacao
½ ounce cream or milk

Briskly shake all ingredients with ice in a cocktail shaker, strain over fresh ice in a rocks glass.

Bourbon

THE CLASSICS

BOURBON AND BRANCH

2 ounces bourbon
spring water

Pour bourbon over ice in a rocks glass. Top with a splash of water.

BOURBON AND GINGER ALE

2 ounces bourbon
ginger ale

Fill a highball glass with ice, add bourbon, top with soda and stir.

BOURBON OLD FASHIONED

2 ounces bourbon
1 teaspoon superfine sugar
2 dashes bitters
club soda or seltzer

Muddle sugar, bitters and a splash of soda or seltzer in an Old Fashioned glass using a muddler or the back of a spoon. When sugar is dissolved, fill glass with ice, add bourbon and top off with soda or seltzer. Twist a strip of lemon zest and drop in — or use a slice of orange and a maraschino cherry.

BOURBON TODDY

1½ ounces bourbon
1 teaspoon superfine sugar
3 cloves
cinnamon stick
slice of lemon
boiling water

Place sugar, cloves, cinnamon and lemon slice in a warmed mug. Stir in 1 ounce of boiling water, stir, let stand for two minutes. Add bourbon, top off with more boiling water, stir and dust with grated nutmeg.

MINT JULEP

1½ ounces bourbon
2 teaspoons superfine sugar
6 fresh mint leaves
2½ ounces bourbon

With a muddler or the back of a spoon, muddle mint, sugar and 1½ ounces of bourbon in a cup and let it marinate for one hour. Pour mixture into a highball glass, fill with crushed ice, add remaining 2½ ounces of bourbon. Stir lightly and garnish with a fresh mint leaf. *Note: Purists place the finished julep in the freezer for 30 minutes before serving.*

BALTIMORE ORIOLE

1½ ounces bourbon
½ ounce Cointreau
1 ounce orange juice

Combine ingredients in a shaker with ice, shake briskly, strain into a rocks glass over fresh ice. Garnish with a lemon twist.

BUFFALO SWEAT

1½ ounces bourbon
dash Tabasco sauce

Pour bourbon into a shot glass, add Tabasco.

BOURBON AND COKE

1½ ounces bourbon
cola

Fill a highball glass with ice, add bourbon, top off with cold cola and garnish with a lime wedge.

BROKEN LEG

1½ ounces bourbon
4 ounces hot cider
4 raisins
cinnamon stick
lemon slice
ground cinnamon

Pour ingredients into a warmed mug, stir and dust with ground cinnamon.

CREAM PUNCH

1½ ounces bourbon
2½ ounces cream or milk
1 dash vanilla extract
1 teaspoon superfine sugar

Combine in a shaker with ice, shake briskly, strain over fresh ice in a highball glass. Garnish with a sprinkle of grated nutmeg.

EGGNOG

1½ ounces bourbon
1 whole egg
1 tablespoon powdered sugar
4 ounces cream or milk

Combine ingredients with ice in a cocktail shaker, shake briskly, strain over fresh ice in a highball glass. Dust with grated nutmeg.

FRISCO

1½ ounce bourbon
1 ounce Benedictine

Combine ingredients with ice in a mixing glass, stir thoroughly, strain into a chilled Martini glass. Garnish with a twist.

KENTUCKY COOLER

1½ ounce bourbon
½ ounce rum
1 teaspoon orange juice
1 teaspoon lemon juice
1 dash grenadine

Combine ingredients with ice in a cocktail shaker, shake briskly, strain over fresh ice in a chilled Martini glass.

KING COLE

2 ounces bourbon
1 dash Fernet Branca
1 teaspooon superfine sugar
1 slice orange
1 slice pinaple

Muddle fruit, sugar, Fernet Branca and 1 ounce bourbon in an Old Fashioned glass. Fill glass with ice, add remaining 1½ ounces bourbon and stir lightly.

KOJAK

1½ ounces bourbon
1 ounce passion fruit juice
½ ounce pineapple juice
1 dash dark rum

Combine ingredients with ice in a cocktail shaker, shake briskly, strain over crushed ice in a chilled wine goblet.

LIKE OTHER ARTS, THE ART OF DISTILLATION SPREAD NIMBLY FROM CULTURE TO CULTURE. THE EUROPEANS LEARNED IT FROM THE NORTH AFRICANS DURING THE CRUSADES OF THE 12TH CENTURY.

MAPLE LEAF

1½ ounce bourbon
1 teaspoon maple syrup
juice of ½ lemon

Combine ingredients in a rocks glass filled with ice and stir well.

MILLIONAIRE

1½ ounces bourbon
1 ounce curaçao
1 egg white
1 dash grenadine

Combine ingredients with ice in a cocktail shaker, shake briskly, strain into a chilled cocktail glass or wine goblet.

NEW ORLEANS

1½ ounces bourbon
1 dash orange bitter
2 dashes Angostura bitters
1 dash anisette
2 dashes Pernod
½ teaspoon superfine sugar

Combine ingredients with ice in a mixing glass, stir thoroughly, strain over fresh ice in a rocks glass. Garnish with a twist.

NOCTURNAL

2 ounces bourbon
1 ounce dark crème de cacao
½ ounce cream or milk

Combine ingredients with ice in a cocktail shaker, shake briskly, strain over fresh ice in a rocks glass.

PERFECT MANHATTAN

2 ounces bourbon
½ ounce dry vermouth
½ ounce sweet vermouth
1 dash Angostura bitters

Combine ingredients with ice in a mixing glass, stir thoroughly, strain over fresh ice in an Old Fashioned glass. *Note: In bartending, the term "perfect" denotes the use of equal amounts of sweet and dry vermouth. Hence, a "Perfect Martini" or a "Perfect Manhattan."*

SAZERAC

1½ ounces bourbon
1 dash Pernod
1 dash bitters
1 teaspoon superfine sugar

Combine ingredients in a mixing glass and stir thoroughly. Strain into a rocks glass over fresh ice. Garnish with a lemon twist.

SCARLET RIBBON

1½ ounces bourbon
½ ounce cranberry juice
1 ounce grapefruit juice
1 teaspoon superfine sugar

Combine ingredients with ice in a cocktail shaker, shake briskly, strain into a chilled Martini glass.

SISTERS

1½ ounces bourbon
1½ ounces brandy
1 teaspoon lemon juice
1 teaspoon Grand Marnier

Combine ingredients with ice in a mixing glass, stir thoroughly, strain into a chilled Martini glass.

SPARKLING JULEP

3 ounces bourbon
6 mint leaves
1 teaspoon superfine sugar
1 teaspoon water
sparkling white wine

In a mixing glass, muddle mint, sugar and water using a muddler or the back of a spoon. When sugar is dissolved, add bourbon, stir well and pour over crushed ice in a chilled wine goblet. Top off with sparkling wine and garnish with a sprig of mint.

SUMMER BOURBON

1½ ounces bourbon
3 ounces orange juice
pinch of salt

Combine ingredients with ice in a mixing glass, stir well and strain over crushed ice in a highball glass or a chilled wine goblet.

Other Whiskies

THE CLASSICS

MANHATTAN

2 ounces blended whiskey
½ ounce sweet vermouth
1 dash bitters

Combine ingredients in a mixing glass filled with ice and stir thoroughly. Strain into a Martini glass or over fresh ice in a rocks glass, garnish with a twist and a cherry.

OLD FASHIONED

1 teaspoon superfine sugar or one sugar cube
2 dashes bitters
club soda or seltzer
1½ ounces blended whiskey

With a muddler or the back of a spoon, muddle sugar, bitters and a splash of club soda or seltzer in a rocks or Old Fashioned glass. Fill glass with ice, add whiskey, top off with club soda or seltzer, stir lightly.

WHISKEY HIGHBALL

1½ ounces blended whiskey
club soda, seltzer or ginger ale

Fill a highball glass with ice, add whiskey, top with club soda, seltzer or ginger ale, stir lightly.

WHISKEY SOUR

1½ ounces blended whiskey
½ ounce lemon juice
1 teaspoon superfine sugar

Pour lemon juice over sugar in a short glass and mix until sugar is dissolved. Pour into a cocktail shaker filled with ice and add the whiskey; shake briskly for thorough aeration and serve in a wine or saucer glass. It can also be poured over fresh ice in a rocks glass, and garnished with a cherry. *Note: In place of fresh lemon and sugar you may use a prepared sweet and sour mix, available in bottles at liquor stores.*

ALGONQUIN

1½ ounces blended whiskey
1 ounce dry vermouth
1 ounce pineapple juice

Briskly shake ingredients in a cocktail shaker and strain into a Martini glass.

BLACK AND TAN

1½ ounces Irish whiskey
1 ounce dark Jamaican rum
½ ounce lime juice
1 teaspoon superfine sugar
ginger ale

Combine whiskey, rum, lime juice and sugar in a shaker, shake briskly, strain over fresh ice in a Collins glass. Top off with ginger ale.

BLINKER

1½ ounces blended whiskey
2 ounces grapefruit juice
1 ounce grenadine

Combine ingredients with ice in a cocktail shaker and shake briskly. Strain into a highball glass over fresh ice.

BLOODY MOLLY

2 ounces Irish whiskey
2 to 3 ounces tomato juice
1 dash lemon juice
1 dash Tabasco
1 dash worcestershire sauce
1 pinch fresh horseradish

Combine ingredients in a mixing glass with several ice cubes. Stir thoroughly and strain over fresh ice in a Collins glass.

DISTILLED SPIRITS WERE ONCE TESTED FOR STRENGTH BY MIXING THEM WITH GUNPOWDER AND IGNITING THEM. IT THEY FLARED UP, THEY WERE TOO STRONG; IF THEY BURNED FITFULLY, THEY WERE TOO WEAK. IF THEY BURNED EVENLY, THEY "PROVED OUT." HENCE THE NAME *FIREWATER*.

BOILERMAKER

2 ounces blended whiskey
ice cold beer

Pour whiskey into a shot glass and beer into a chilled Pilsner glass. Serve side by side. Drink the shot of whiskey first and follow with a beer chaser.

BROOKLYN

1½ ounces rye
1½ ounces sweet vermouth
2 dashes orange bitters
1 dash maraschino liqueur

Fill a rocks glass with ice, add ingredients, stir lightly.

DE RIGUEUR

2 ounces blended whiskey
1 ounce grapefruit juice
1 ounce honey

Briskly shake ingredients with ice in a cocktail shaker and strain into a highball glass over fresh ice.

EARTHQUAKE

1½ ounces blended whiskey
1½ ounces gin
1½ ounces Pernod

Briskly shake ingredients with ice in a cocktail shaker, strain into a highball glass over fresh ice.

GLOOM LIFTER

2 ounces blended whiskey
½ ounce lemon juice
1 teaspoon superfine sugar
½ egg white

Pour ingredients over ice in a cocktail shaker. Shake briskly and strain into a rocks glass over fresh ice.

HORSE'S NECK

1½ ounces blended whiskey
1 large lemon twist
1 dash Angostura bitters
ginger ale

Pour ingredients over ice in a Collins glass, stir.

MAPLE LEAF

1½ ounces Canadian whiskey
1 teaspoon lemon juice
1 teaspoon maple syrup

Briskly shake ingredients in a cocktail shaker with ice, strain into a cocktail glass.

NEW YORK COCKTAIL

2½ ounces blended whiskey
½ teaspoon superfine sugar
1 dash grenadine
1 ounce lemon juice

Briskly shake ingredients in a shaker with ice, strain into a Martini glass, and garnish with a lemon twist.

OLD PAL

1 ounce rye
1 ounce dry vermouth
1 ounce Campari

Pour ingredients over ice in a mixing glass, stir well, strain over fresh ice in a rocks glass.

PICK-UP

2 ounces blended whiskey
1 ounce Femet Branca
3 dashes Pernod

Pour ingredients over ice in a mixing glass, stir well, strain over fresh ice in a rocks glass. Garnish with a lemon slice.

RATTLESNAKE

1½ ounces blended whiskey
1 teaspoon lemon juice
1 teaspoon sugar
1 egg white
¼ teaspoon Pernod

Pour ingredients into cocktail shaker filled with ice. Shake vigorously, strain over fresh ice in a rocks glass.

"A FRIEND AND I ONCE EMPLOYED A MATHEMATICIAN TO FIGURE OUT HOW MANY COCKTAILS COULD BE FASHIONED OF THE *MATERIA BIBULICA* ORDINARILY AVAILABLE AT A FIRST-CLASS BAR. HE REPORTED THAT THE NUMBER WAS 17,864,392,788. WE TRIED 273 AT RANDOM AND FOUND THEM ALL GOOD, THOUGH SOME, OF COURSE, WERE BETTER THAN OTHERS."

~H. L. MENCKEN

T.N.T.

1½ ounces blended whiskey
1½ ounces Pernod

Briskly shake ingredients in a cocktail shaker with ice, strain into a rocks glass.

WHISKEY MINT

1 teaspoon superfine sugar
4 fresh mint leaves
club soda
1½ ounces blended whiskey

Muddle sugar, mint leaves and a dash of soda in the bottom of an Old Fashioned glass. Fill glass with ice, add whiskey and top with club soda. Garnish with a sprig of mint.

WILD-EYED ROSE

3 ounces Irish whiskey
1 ounce grenadine
juice of lime half
club soda

Fill a highball glass with ice, add ingredients and stir lightly.

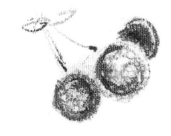

BRANDY & LIQUEURS

*W*ater of life. In its earliest form, that was the name for brandy, a liquor distilled from the juice of fermented fruit, usually grapes. In the Middle Ages, the French wine growers learned that they could reduce the duty they paid on exported wine if they lowered its volume by distilling it into a colorless spirit which they called *eau-de-vie*, or "water of life". Brandy is actually a shortened form of brandywine, from the Dutch *brandewijn*, meaning "burnt" or distilled wine.

The finest of the brandies are Cognac and Armagnac from France. Cognac is produced in a small area surrounding the town of Cognac in the Charentes region of western France. It is double distilled in copper pot stills and aged for at least five years, and usually longer, in casks of Limousin oak. The cognac is then blended and bottled, at which point the aging process stops. The Cognac-producing area is divided into seven sections, the most prestigious of which are Grande Champagne and Petite Champagne. These terms refer to areas of open space, and have no connection with the Champagne district of France where bubbly wine is produced.

Armagnac is produced in Gascony in southwestern France from the same kinds of grapes, but under different growing conditions. Armagnac is distilled only once, resulting in a characteristically earthy, pungent flavor.

The finest Cognacs and Armagnacs should be sipped straight, from a snifter, so that one can appreciate their aroma and color. Less prestigious brandies and cognacs can still be very tasty, and are excellent in mixed drinks. Other countries that produce good brandies include Spain, Portugal, Greece, Germany, and Peru, where Pisco brandy is made.

The United States is the second largest producer of brandies after France, and California produces the great majority of American brandies. Most are produced in column stills, and by law they must be aged at least two years in oak. California brandies make excellent mixers.

In France brandy is also distilled from *pomace*, the stems and skins of grapes that remain after pressing. This colorless, unaged brandy, known as *marc*, has quite a strong flavor. *Grappa*, the Italian version of brandy distilled from pomace, tends to have a harsher taste.

Brandies are produced from other fruits as well as grapes. Known as *alcools blancs*, or "white alcohols," they are colorless and usually unaged. These include kirsch, made from cherries; mirabelle, from plums; framboise, from raspberries; and poire Williams from pears. Slivovitz is a plum brandy made in the Balkans. Calvados is French apple brandy, distilled from cider in pot stills and aged from 4 to 20 years. American applejack, also made from fermented apple juice, dates back to colonial times; it retains the perfume of apples, and is aged in wood at least two years.

LIQUEURS AND CORDIALS

Liqueurs (also known as cordials) are made by adding flavorings from fruits, flowers, herbs, spices, roots, seeds, and barks to a base of brandy or other spirits. They are sweetened with sugar at least 2-1/2 percent by weight, and vary in proof from low to quite high. Liqueurs contribute unique flavor characteristics to many mixed drinks.

Some liqueurs are generic, based on single flavors, while others are proprietary, based on secret formulas which often have colorful histories.

FLAVORED BRANDIES

Flavored brandies are a class of liqueurs in the U.S. that are made with a brandy base, sweetened with at least 2.5 percent sugar, and flavored. They are bottled at no less than 70 proof, higher than many liqueurs. Examples are peach-flavored brandy, cherry-flavored brandy, ginger-flavored brandy, and coffee-flavored brandy. These flavored brandies are not to be confused with the clear, unsweetened fruit brandies distilled from the juices of fruits.

A LIQUEUR LEXICON

AMARETTO *flavored with almond from almond pits*

ANISETTE *licorice flavor from aniseed*

BENEDICTINE *based on Cognac and herbs; created by Benedictine monks in 1510*

CHARTREUSE *made by the Carthusian Brothers in France since 1605; spicy, aromatic flavor with a brandy base; yellow Chartreuse is 86 proof, and green Chartreuse is 110 proof, high for a liqueur*

CHERRY HEERING *an outstanding cherry liqueur, produced in Copenhagen, Denmark*

COINTREAU *a cognac-based Curaçao liqueur*

CURAÇAO *generic name for liqueurs made from the dried peel of bitter Curaçao oranges*

CRÈME DE CAÇAO *white or brown; chocolate flavored, from cacao and vanilla beans*

CRÈME DE CAFE *coffee flavored*

CRÈME DE CASSIS *flavored with black currants*

CRÈME DE NOYAUX *almond taste from apricot and peach pits*

CRÈME DE MENTHE *peppermint flavor; may be white or green*

DRAMBUIE *rich liqueur from Scotch malt whiskey and heather honey (reputedly based on a recipe brought to Scotland in 1745 by an attendant of Bonnie Prince Charlie)*

FRANGELICO *hazelnut flavored liqueur*

GRAND MARNIER *a fine cognac-based Curaçao*

KAHLUA *Mexican coffee liqueur made from coffee beans, cacao, vanilla, and brandy*

KIRSH *liqueur made from cherries*

KÜMMEL *distilled from grain, flavored with caraway and cumin seeds*

LIQUORE GALLIANO OR GALLIANO *yellow in color; spicy and aromatic flavor of herbs and flowers*

MARASCHINO *from the Marasca cherry*

SAMBUCA *clear liqueur with heavy licorice flavor*

SLOE GIN *made with sloe berries steeped in gin*

SOUTHERN COMFORT LIQUEUR *high-proof liqueur based on bourbon and peaches*

STREGA *yellow color; sweet and spicy flavor*

TIA MARIA *coffee liqueur from Jamaica, with rum base*

TRIPLE SEC *white Curaçao; higher proof than orange Curaçao*

Brandy & Liqueurs

Brandy, cognacs and liqueurs are often served straight, at room temperature, and handsomely repay the use of proper glassware. The glass should be bell-shaped, curving in at the top, which helps trap the aroma of the liqueur. An especially nice touch is to heat the glass first with a swirl of hot water, since heat promotes the aromatic qualities as well.

B AND B

1 ounce brandy
1 ounce Benedictine

Pour brandy and Benedictine into a cordial glass, or over ice in a rocks glass. *Note: B & B is available in a bottle, premixed by the makers of Benedictine.*

B-52

1 ounce orange liqueur
1 ounce coffee liqueur
1 ounce Irish cream liqueur

Pour over ice in a rocks glass.

BEAUTIFUL

2 ounces cognac
1 ounce orange liqueur

Pour a little hot water into a snifter to warm it. Pour out the water and add the cognac and liqueur.

BETWEEN THE SHEETS

1½ ounces brandy
1½ ounces Cointreau
1½ ounces light rum

Combine ingredients with four ice cubes in a cocktail shaker, shake briskly, strain into a high ball glass over fresh ice.

BOCCE BALL

1½ ounces Amaretto
3 ounces cold orange juice
club soda or seltzer

Fill a highball glass with ice, add Amaretto and orange juice, top off with club soda or seltzer, stir lightly.

BRANDY ALEXANDER

1½ ounces brandy
1 ounce white crème de cacao
1 ounce cream or milk
grated nutmeg

Combine ingredients with ice in a shaker, shake briskly, strain into a Martini glass and grate nutmeg over it.

BRANDY FLIP

1½ ounces brandy
1 egg
1 teaspoon sugar
2 teaspoons cream or milk

Combine ingredients with ice in a cocktail shaker, shake very briskly, strain into a rocks glass over fresh ice.

SUGAR'S SWEET INTENSITY HAS APPARENTLY APPEALED IMMEDIATELY WHEREVER IT WAS AVAILABLE TO HUMAN SOCIETY. SUGAR CANE WAS FIRST CARRIED TO THE NEW WORLD BY COLUMBUS FROM THE SPANISH CANARY ISLANDS IN 1493 AND IN THE 16TH CENTURY, EUROPEANS COVETED SUGAR AS A LUXURY, MEDICINE, AND SPICE. BY 1750 THE POOREST ENGLISH FARM LABORER'S WIFE TOOK SUGAR IN HER TEA. IN THE 1990S, THE AVERAGE U.S. CITIZEN CONSUMES OVER 100 POUNDS OF SUGAR EACH YEAR.

GRASSHOPPER

1 ounce green crème de menthe
1 ounce white crème de cacao
1 ounce cream or milk

Combine ingredients with ice in a cocktail shaker, shake very briskly, strain into a cocktail glass.

SIDECAR

2 ounces cognac
1 ounce Grand Marnier
½ ounce lemon juice

Combine ingredients with ice in a cocktail shaker, shake very briskly, strain into a cocktail glass.

SLOE GIN FIZZ

3 ounces sloe gin
1 ounce lemon juice
1 teaspoon superfine sugar
club soda or seltzer

Combine sloe gin, lemon juice and sugar with ice in a cocktail shaker, shake briskly, strain into a Collins glass over fresh ice. Top off with club soda or seltzer.

STINGER

2 ounces brandy
½ ounce white crème de menthe

Combine ingredients with ice in a mixing glass, stir thoroughly, strain into a Martini glass, or serve over ice in a rocks glass.

Homemade Liqueurs

IRISH CREAM LIQUEUR

*4 cups Irish whiskey, 2 14-ounce cans sweetened condensed milk,
¼ teaspoon almond extract, 1 ounce semisweet chocolate, melted and
cooled, 2 teaspoons vanilla extract, 6 eggs, 2 cups light cream.*

Blend all ingredients until smooth, pour into glass
bottle and cap tightly and refrigerate. Let the flavors
blend for at least two weeks before using, but drink within
six weeks.

COFFEE LIQUEUR

*4 cups freshly brewed strong espresso, 8 cups sugar, 3 cups vodka,
2 cups brandy, 2 whole vanilla beans.*

Mix well, being sure to dissolve sugar. Store in dark,
cool place for 30 days before using.

RAISIN BRANDY

Seedless raisins, brandy.

Add seedless raisins to a large glass jar or decanter until
it is approximately three-quarters full. Pour in as much
brandy as the jar will contain. Stopper and set aside in a
dark, cool place for several weeks.

CHOCOLATE CREAM LIQUEUR

*4 cups brandy, 2 14-ounce cans sweetened condensed milk, 6
ounces semisweet chocolate, melted and cooled, 2 teaspoons vanilla
extract, 6 eggs, 2 cups light cream.*

Blend all ingredients until smooth, pour into glass
bottle and cap tightly and refrigerate. Let the flavors
blend for at least two weeks before using, but drink within
six weeks.

After-Dinner Drinks

Keep the dinner conversation pleasantly aloft with a slight change of key by offering after-dinner liqueurs, cordials, and brandies. Bring a trayful of colorful choices, in their handsome bottles, directly to the table and let guests choose their favorites. Provide an assortment of cordial glasses and snifters and a platter of rich cookies. Or serve each guest a dish of chocolate-nut or honey-vanilla ice cream and present a trayful of liqueurs at the same time: guests can pour their favorite liqueurs over ice cream for a simple and delicious dessert. Garnish, if desired, with flavored whipped cream, cookies, chopped toasted nuts, or sprigs of mint.

CHAMPAGNE &
WINE DRINKS

"I am drinking stars!"

DOM PERIGNON

ixing the noble grape. As more and more
Americans learn to appreciate fine wines,
they are also discovering what has been
known since ancient times — that wine
is an excellent mixer. Not only the
stronger distilled spirits, but also wine, champagne, and flavored and
fortified wines, are important ingredients in creative drink making.

Of course the finest champagnes and wines should never be used for
mixing, but there is a world of more modest table wines and less
illustrious champagnes that make a perfect contribution to a wide range
of coolers, cocktails, punches, and party drinks.

CHAMPAGNE

"I am drinking stars!" exclaimed Dom Perignon, a blind Benedictine monk of seventeenth-century France. According to tradition, the ecstatic Dom had just tasted a new kind of wine produced in the cellars of his monastery — a wine alive with tiny bubbles.

Champagne's unique carbonation is the result of a second fermentation which takes place in the bottle. A "dose" of sugar is introduced into a bottle of wine, which is sealed with a temporary cork. After the wine has fermented and become bubbly, the cork is removed together with collected sediments. The small empty space in the bottle is refilled with a dosage of sugar soaked in still wine, and the bottle is deftly recorked. The amount of sugar in the dosage determines the kind of champagne. From lowest to highest sugar content, these are *brut, extra sec* or *extra dry, sec* or *dry, demi sec,* and *doux,* for the sweetest.

The only bubbly wine that can be called champagne is that produced in the French province of the same name. Others, even if they look and taste like champagne, are really sparkling wines made by the *methode champenoise.* Some lesser sparkling wines undergo their second fermentation in large tanks by a bulk method. Still others are produced by injecting carbon dioxide into a white wine before bottling.

The very finest champagnes should never be used as mixers. They should be drunk chilled, in tall flute glasses, not in the shallow bowl-shaped glasses that allow the bubbles to dissipate.

When used in mixed drinks, sparkling wines should be as cold as possible. Be careful to stir the mixture very gently, so as not to dissipate the precious sparkle.

WINE

It would be far too ambitious to attempt a discussion of wines in this book, since we are concerned here with their use in mixed drinks. The best wines in the world unquestionably come from France. In the late 1870s, the French vines were all but eradicated by an epidemic of the phylloxera plant louse. To protect the noble *vitis vinifera* vines, they were grafted onto American root stock, and these grafted vines are now raised throughout the world, retaining the flavor of the original European grapes.

Some great wines are produced today in California, side by side with humbler wines that are ideal for daily consumption with meals or for mixing. Other American wines of note are produced in New York, Ohio, Oregon, and Washington State. Italy produces some sublime wines as well as more ordinary table wines, and some of the white wines of Germany are highly prized. Spain, Australia, Chile, and Argentina also produce excellent wines. The flavoring and sweetening of wine is an ancient practice, originally done partly to improve the flavor of young wines, or to preserve them from spoilage. In ancient Greece, Hippocrates invented a concoction of wine sweetened with honey and flavored with cinnamon and other spices. Known as Hippocras, this was a popular drink during the Middle Ages.

The so-called fortified wines have had brandy added to them — to stop fermentation and retain sweetness, in the case of port (from Portugal); and to increase the alcoholic content, in the case of sherry (from Spain) and Madeira (from the Portuguese island of Madeira). Aromatic aperitif wines such as Dubonnet, St. Raphael, Lillet and Byrrh, continue the long tradition of flavoring, sweetening, and fortifying wines. These flavored wines are important constituents of many mixed drinks.

Champagne

ALFONSO

1 ounce Dubonnet
1 dash bitters
1 sugar cube
chilled champagne

Place sugar in a champagne saucer glass and sprinkle with bitters. Add one ice cube, fill with champagne and garnish with a lemon twist.

AMBROSIA

3 ounces brandy
3 ounces apple brandy
1 teaspoon raspberry syrup, or to taste
champagne

Combine brandies and syrup with four ice cubes in a cocktail shaker and shake vigorously. Strain into two chilled wine glasses. Top off with champagne. Stir very gently. *Serves two.*

AMERICANA

1 teaspoon bourbon
1 dash orange bitters
½ teaspoon superfine sugar
chilled champagne

Combine bourbon, bitters and sugar in a rocks glass and stir well. Pour into a champagne flute and top off with champagne.

BLACK VELVET

cold stout
chilled champagne

Fill half a champagne flute with stout. Slowly fill rest of flute with champagne.

CHAMPAGNE COCKTAIL

1 sugar cube
1 dash Angostura bitters
1 lemon twist
chilled champagne

Add a few drops of bitters to a cube of sugar and drop it into a fluted glass. Add champagne and a lemon twist. The bubbles will slowly melt the sugar and bitters as they travel up the flute.

CHAMPAGNE COOLER

1 ounce brandy
1 ounce Cointreau
chilled champagne

Half fill a highball glass with ice, add brandy and Cointreau, slowly top off with champagne and garnish with a sprig of mint.

CHICAGO

1½ ounces brandy
4 drops Triple Sec
2 dashes Angostura bitters
chilled champagne

Dampen and dip rim of a wine glass with sugar. Briskly shake brandy, Triple Sec and bitters with four ice cubes in a cocktail shaker, strain into wine glass, slowly top off with champagne.

FRENCH 75

1½ ounce gin
1½ ounces lemon juice
2 teaspoons superfine sugar
chilled champagne

Combine gin, lemon juice and sugar in a Collins glass and stir well until sugar is completely dissolved. Fill glass with ice and top with champagne.

KIR ROYALE

1½ teaspoons crème de cassis
chilled champagne

Pour champagne to fill a flute three-quarters full; add crème de cassis, garnish with a lemon twist.

TOASTING PROBABLY ORIGINATED IN THE MIDDLE AGES, AS A SAFETY PRECAUTION. THE CLINK OF GLASSES WAS THOUGHT TO SCARE AWAY THE DEVIL.

MIMOSA

cold orange juice
chilled champagne

Fill a champagne flute three-quarters full with champagne, top off with orange juice. For a noble variation, add an ounce of cognac.

PEACH TREAT

1 ounce peach brandy
2 ounces orange juice
chilled champagne

Combine brandy and orange juice with four ice cubes in a cocktail shaker, shake briskly, strain into a large wine glass. Slowly top off with champagne and garnish with a peach slice.

REMBRANDT

½ cup fresh stawberries
chilled champagne

Puree stawberries in an electric blender, pour into champagne flute and slowly top off with champagne.

SOYER-AU-CHAMPAGNE

1 tablespoon vanilla ice cream
2 dashes maraschino
2 dashes curaçao
2 dashes brandy
chilled champagne

Place ice cream in a champagne saucer, pour maraschino, curaçao and brandy over ice cream. Slowly top off with champagne.

Wine

WHITE WINE SPRITZER

5 ounces chilled dry white wine

chilled club soda or seltzer

Fill a wine glass with ice, add wine, top off with soda or seltzer and garnish with a twist of lemon.

WINE COLLINS

4 ounces dry red wine
1 teaspoon lime juice
chilled bitter lemon soda

Fill a Collins glass with ice, add wine and lime juice, top off with soda.

KIR

5 ounces chilled white wine
1 teaspoon crème de cassis

Pour wine into wine glass, add crème de cassis and garnish with a lemon twist.

MEDICATO

5 ounces chilled dry white wine

1 teaspoon Campari

Pour wine into a wine glass, add Campari, stir lightly and garnish with an orange twist.

CHABLIS COOLER

4 ounces chilled chablis
1 ounce vodka
2 teaspoons grenadine
2 teaspoons lemon juice
1 dash vanilla extract

Moisten the rim of a Collins glass and dip in a saucer of sugar. Combine ingredients with four cubes of ice in a mixing glass, stir well, strain over fresh ice into the Collins glass.

CORK COMES FROM THE CORK OAK TREE, AN EVERGREEN. IT GROWS ONLY AROUND THE MEDITERRANEAN SEA IN AN AREA ABOUT THE SIZE OF NEW JERSEY WHICH INCLUDES PARTS OF SPAIN, PORTUGAL, AND NORTH AFRICA. TREES MUST BE 40 YEARS OLD BEFORE THEIR BARK IS USEFUL FOR WINE CORKS AND FROM THAT TIME THEY CAN BE HARVESTED EVERY EIGHT TO NINE YEARS WITHOUT INJURY TO THE TREE.

CLARET ORANGEADE

3 ounces cold orange juice
dry red wine

Fill a highball glass with ice, add orange juice, top off with wine and stir lightly.

DRAWBRIDGE

4 ounces dry white wine
1 splash curaçao
club soda or seltzer

Fill a wine glass with ice, add wine and curaçao, top off with soda or seltzer.

L.A. COOLER

½ ounce bourbon
½ ounce banana liqueur
2 teaspoons Cointreau
1 teaspoon lemon juice
2 ounces pineapple juice
3 ounces chilled chablis

Combine bourbon, banana liqueur, Cointreau, lemon juice and pineapple juice with a heaping cup of crushed ice in an electric blender. Blend until smooth, pour into a large wine glass, top off with chilled wine, stir very lightly.

PINEAPPLE COCKTAIL

6 ounces chilled dry white wine
1 cup crushed pineapple
9 ounces sherry
3 ounces pineapple juice
1 tablespoon lemon juice

Combine crushed pineapple and white wine in a large glass pitcher, refrigerate and allow to marinate for two to three hours. Add sherry, pineapple juice and lemon juice, stir well and return to the refrigerator until mixture is well chilled. Serve over ice in rocks glasses and garnish with sticks of fresh pineapple. *Serves six.*

SPIRITED FRUIT DESSERTS ARE PERFECT WITH CHAMPAGNE. FOR A DELICIOUS DESSERT, MARINATE FRESH BERRIES IN EQUAL PARTS VODKA, TRIPLE SEC, AND RUM. SERVE OVER CARAMEL CUSTARD, ICE CREAM, OR SPONGE CAKE.

RED FROST

4 ounces chilled dry red wine
1 teaspoon crème de cassis

Fill a wine glass with ice, add wine, add crème de cassis and garnish with a twist of lemon.

RUSSIAN BLUSH

4 ounces chilled red wine
1 ounce vodka
1 tasblespoon Grand Marnier

Combine all ingredients with four ice cubes in a mixing glass, stir thoroughly, strain over fresh ice in a highball glass.

SAUTERNE COCKTAIL

2 ounces chilled sauterne
3 ounces chilled bitter lemon soda

Fill a highball glass with ice, add wine and soda and garnish with a twist of lemon.

7-UP COOLER

4 ounces red burgundy
chilled 7-Up

Fill a highball galss with ice, add wine, top off with 7-Up, stir lightly.

WHENCE THE COCKTAIL? ACCORDING TO ONE OF MANY THEORIES, THE WORD DERIVES FROM *COQUETIER* — FRENCH FOR "EGG CUP" — THE CONTAINER USED BY ANTOINE PEYCHAUD FOR HIS SMALL POTENT CONCOCTIONS POPULAR WITH CITIZENS OF NEW ORLEANS AROUND 1800. OTHERS TRACE THE WORD TO 1600, WHEN ENGLISH SOLDIERS STATIONED IN THE GULF OF MEXICO EXTENDED THEIR RUM RATIONS BY MIXING THEM WITH LOCAL LIQUORS. THEY STIRRED THE DRINK WITH A *COLA DE GALLO*, A STEM OF THE PLANT WHOSE NAME TRANSLATES AS "COCK'S TAIL."

COFFEE & COFFEE DRINKS

"According to an advertisement in the LONDON PUBLICK
ADVISER *of 19 May 1657, coffee was 'a very wholesome
and Physical drink' that 'helpeth Digestion, quickeneth
the Spirits, maketh the heart lightsom, is good against
Eye-sores, Coughs, or Colds, Rhumes, Consumption,
Heach-ach, Dropsie. . . and many others.'*

REAY TANNAHILL

*I*t is likely that coffee originated in the mountains
of Ethiopia and was cultivated as early as the 6th
century. Modern coffee, an infusion of the roasted
beans, was invented in the 13th century. It is said to have found early
intense popularity among the Muslims, especially the sect known as
"whirling" dervishes. The name we use for this aromatic stimulant comes
originally from Arabic the *qahwah*, which originally meant "wine"

through the Turkish word *kahveh*. Coffee was the wine of the muslims, who abstained from real wine because of religious proscription. By 1554 the fashion had spread to Constantinople, where the first coffee house was established.

In Europe, coffee houses — which eventually would evolve into Europe's beloved cafes — became very popular in the 17th century. Throughout the century the traders of the Near East continued to control the coffee market, but during the colonial period that followed, alternative sources were established. The Dutch discovered that coffee would grow in their territories in Java, and later they introduced cultivation of the bean to Sri Lanka (Ceylon). The English encouraged coffee cultivation in the West Indies. A study of the evolution of coffee cultivation and the coffee trade reads with the intense drama, power politics, and complex relationships characteristic of the most telling passages of human history.

Venerable coffee, for many, is the perfect finale to a great evening. A round of delicious coffee drinks can encourage good dinner conversation to continue after the last plate and serving bowl has left the table.

For coffee drinks, you may wish to acquire heat-resistant glasses, often known as "Irish coffee" glasses; practical little showcases for the beauties of coffee. Preheat coffee glasses, mugs, or cups with hot water so that liquor and cream won't lower the temperature of the completed drink. Use real whipping cream for coffee toppings.

There are many luscious coffee drinks, using a great range of flavors and ingredients, but their common foundation is good brewed coffee. Start with high-quality coffee ground appropriately for your coffee making method. Of the several coffee species, two dominate: *Coffea arabica*, the finest coffee, and *Coffea canephora* (popularly known as *Robusta*), the most common because of its larger yield and hardier nature. Most commercial-grade grocery store coffee sold in vacuum cans is made from *Robusta* beans;

most coffee custom-roasted and sold by gourmet coffee merchants contains *Arabica* beans.

Green coffee beans can be roasted to several stages of doneness. The more the beans are roasted, the darker their color and stronger their flavor will be. The four basic stages of roasting from lightest to darkest are American, Viennese, French, and Italian. Light American roast has been the traditonal preference of coffee drinkers in many parts of the U. S. (dependent somewhat on locale), but the darker "European roasts" are gaining popularity. French roast is just right for cafe au lait and Italian is the roast for espresso.

If possible, it is best to buy your coffee beans from a familiar merchant who custom roasts them and to grind them yourself immediately before brewing your coffee. Water for coffeemaking should be fresh and cold. Once a pot is brewed, it should remain on the heating plate no more than half an hour, after which it begins to become bitter.

Store whole roasted beans in an airtight container away from the light, if storing for a few weeks; for longer storage, freeze them. Ground coffee exposed to air can begin to lose flavor within hours or days. For storage up to two weeks, keep it in an airtight container in the refrigerator. Fineness of grind should be appropriate to your coffee-making method: a less fine grind is best for automatic drip brewers and very finely ground coffee is used for espresso. Most coffee lovers do not recommend the use of a percolator because its intense heat can make coffee bitter, but coffee for percolators is the least fine grind. If you grind your own coffee, use a dry brush to whisk out the grinder after each use to avoid stale residual coffee grounds. Evenly ground coffee infuses best.

Most of the delicious coffee drinks that follow will benefit from well-made European roast coffee.

How Coffee is Classified

PLACE OF ORIGIN

Arabian: A collection of various coffees. Once this group included Mocha, shipped from a port by the same name, and known for its mellowness and low acidity. It was traditionally blended with the more acidic Java coffee to make an excellent blend called Mocha-Java. Today, however, most Arabian coffee is high in acidity and low in mellowness. The exact formula depends on the blender.

Brazilian: Brazil is the world's largest coffee producer but its coffee is not the most highly favored by aficionados. Brazilian Bourbon Santos is sometimes blended with good-quality, high-acid coffee.

Caribbean: The best Caribbean coffee beans come from Jamaica, the origin of Blue Mountain coffee, a superb — and very expensive — full-bodied coffee. Good coffees also come from Cuba, Haiti, and the Dominican Republic.

Central American: Rich, sound-bodied, sufficiently acid beans come from Costa Rica, Guatemala, Honduras, El Salvador, and Nicaragua.

Columbia: Columbian Supremo is the favorite.

Hawaiian: Kona coffee is cultivated in a relatively small area and hence is quite expensive. It varies from year to year but in good years is excellent.

Indian: Southern India produces many coffees, including those of Malabar.

Indonesian: The island of Java, Sulawesa islands and Bali produce excellent coffees though lower in acid than most.

Other coffee growing areas: Mexico and many areas in Africa.

TYPE OF ROAST

American: Lightest roast. Typically used for American coffee.

Viennese: Slightly darker. A good choice for after-dinner coffee.

French: Darker. Best for coffee drinks to which cream or milk will be added.

Italian: The darkest roast. A must for a good cup of espresso.

FLAVORED COFFEES

The classic New Orleans chicory coffee is made by infusing dark-roast coffee with the dried ground root of the chicory plant.

Many flavored coffee beans are now on the market — vanilla, chocolate, raspberry, mint, cinnamon, and others. In general, these are made by rolling the still-warm just-roasted beans in natural or processed flavorings.

Whipped Creams

CINNAMON CREAM

½ cup heavy cream, 1 teaspoon sugar, ¼ teaspoon ground cinnamon

Whip cream with whisk or electric mixer until soft peaks form. Add sugar and cinnamon and beat until stiff. Makes one cup.

CHOCOLATE CREAM

½ cup heavy cream, 1 tablespoon sugar, 2 tablespoons unsweetened cocoa

Combine sugar and cocoa. Whip cream with whisk or electric mixer until soft peaks form. Add cocoa mixture and beat until stiff. Makes two cups.

BRANDIED CREAM

½ cup heavy cream, 1 tablespoon sugar, 2 tablespoons brandy or flavored brandy

Whip cream with whisk or electric mixer until soft peaks form. Add brandy and beat until stiff. Makes about one cup.

HONEY-NUTMEG CREAM

½ cup heavy cream, 2 tablespoons honey, ¼ teaspoon grated nutmeg

Whip cream with whisk or electric mixer until soft peaks form. Add honey and nutmeg and beat until stiff. Makes about one cup. *Note: If possible, obtain whole nutmegs and grate them yourself rather than using the commercial powdered version.*

Iced Coffee

One of the splendid joys of summer is a tall, frosted glass of iced coffee, marbelized with cream. Watch before stirring and enjoy the view. And why shouldn't iced coffee be joined with spirits? Because ice will inevitably dilute it, iced coffee must start double-strength, and preferably be made from rich dark-roasted beans. Make the coffee ahead of time and chill it. You may wish to sweeten the coffee while it is still hot enough to dissolve the sugar. For spiced coffee as a base, steep the hot coffee with cinnamon sticks, cloves, and allspice berries.

Then fill tall frosted glasses with very cold coffee, add plenty of ice, and embellish with brandy, cognac, or any of your favorite liqueurs. Garnish with mint, lemon, a cinnamon stick. Pass the cream and sugar.

Coffee Drinks

ALMOND COFFEE

4 ounces strong black coffee
1 ounce Amaretto liqueur
whipped cream
toasted almond slivers

Add Amaretto to coffee, top with cream, sprinkle with almond slivers.

ALMOND MOCHA

1 cup strong black coffee
4 teaspoons sugar
6 tablespoons almond liqueur (such as Amaretto)
2 tablespoons unsweetened cocoa, preferably Dutch process
½ teaspoon ground cinnamon
⅔ cup milk (optional)
pinch salt
Cinnamon Whipped Cream

Stir coffee, sugar, and liqueur together in a saucepan. Combine cocoa, cinnamon and ⅓ cups milk in a small bowl. Add to the coffee mixture with the remaining milk and the salt. Bring to simmer. Pour into mugs and top with Cinnamon Whipped Cream. Garnish with chocolate coffee beans if desired. *Makes two servings.*

CAFE BRÛLOT

1 two-inch cinnamon stick
6 whole cloves
¼ cup thinly slivered orange peel
¼ cup thinly slivered lemon peel
3 lumps sugar
½ cup brandy
2 tablespoons curaçao
3 cups hot strong black coffee

Combine the cinnamon, cloves, orange and lemon peel, and sugar in a chafing dish. Mash together with the back of a ladle. Add brandy and curaçao and mix well. When the mixture begins to boil, light a wooden kitchen match and hold near the mixture to ignite it. Keep stirring to dissolve the sugar. Add the coffee gradually, to keep the flame alive as long as possible. Ladle out into demitasse cups. *Note: This makes a beautiful spectacle when done at the table.*

CAFE ROYAL FRAPPÉ

4 ounces double-strength dark-roasted coffee, at room temperature or chilled
2 ounces cognac
shaved ice

Half fill a cocktail shaker with finely shaved ice. Add coffee and cognac. Shake vigorously and pour into a champagne glass.

CAFE AU CACAO FRAPPÉ

4 ounces double-strength dark-roasted coffee, at room temperature or chilled
4 ounces crème de cacao
shaved ice

Half fill a cocktail shaker with finely shaved ice. Add coffee and creme de cacao. Shake vigorously and pour into a champagne glass.

CAFE ROYAL

one cup hot double-strength dark-roasted coffee
1 tablespoon cognac
1 teaspoon brandy
1 cube of sugar

Float the tablespoon of cognac atop the cup of coffee. Place a sugar cube in a teaspoon and fill the spoon with warm brandy. Hold the spoon just above the coffee to warm the brandy so that it may be ignited. Touch a match to the spoonful of brandy to ignite it, then lower it gently into the coffee. Stir gently until the flame dies.

CONTINENTAL COFFEE

¼ teaspoon coriander
1 teaspoon sugar
¼ cup warmed sweet red wine
2 cups strong hot coffee
orange slices

Add coriander, sugar and wine to brewed coffee. Pour into mug and top with orange slice.

COCOA KISS

4 ounces hot chocolate
2 ounces peppermint schnapps
or 2 ounces crème de menthe
heavy cream, whipped

Pour hot chocolate (made with milk) into a pre-heated mug or glass, add liquors and stir; float whipped cream on top.

COCONUT COMBO

½ ounce each Grand Marnier, Cointreau, Galliano and dark rum
strong hot black coffee
brown sugar
whipped cream
coconut
orange peel
lemon peel

Combine liqueurs and rum in a brandy goblet or mug. Add coffee and brown sugar. Stir. Top with whipped cream and garnish with coconut and citrus peel.

CAFE DE MENTHE

3/4 ounce Kahluah
3/4 ounce crème de menthe
strong hot coffee
whipped cream

Preheat brandy goblet or mug with hot water. Drain. Pour both liqueurs into mug or glass and fill with coffee. Top with cream.

CAFE CHAMBORD

3/4 ounce Chambord
strong hot coffee
whipped cream

Pour Chambord into mug or glass and fill with coffee. Top with cream.

COFFEE KISS

2 ounches crème de cacao
1 ounce crème de menthe or 2 ounces Vandermint Liqueur
4 ounces hot black coffee
1 teaspoon sugar or 1 sugar cube
heavy cream, whipped

Put sugar into a warm mug or heat-resistant glass, add coffee, crème de cacao and crème de menthe or Vandermint Liqueur and stir. Float the cream on top — the more it's whipped, the easier it will be to float it. If you prefer a more liquid cream texture pour it over the back of a spoon held close to the coffee's surface.

HAZELNUT COFFEE

⅓ cup hazelnuts, toasted
2⅓ tablespoons sugar
1 cup heavy cream
2 cups hot strong coffee
¾ cup hazelnut liqueur, such as Frangelico

Finely chop the hazelnuts with one tablespoon of the sugar. Beat cream till soft peaks form, then sift in the chopped nuts, reserving the coarser pieces that stay in the sifter for garnish. Combine the coffee, remaining sugar, and liqueur and divide among four cups or cups. Top each with whipped cream and garnish with reserved chopped nuts. *Serves four.*

IRISH COFFEE

2 ounches Irish whiskey
4 ounces hot black coffee
1 teaspoon sugar or 1 sugar cube
heavy cream, whipped

Put sugar into a warm mug or heat-resistant glass, add coffee and whiskey and stir. Float the cream on top — the more it's whipped, the easier it will be to float it. If you prefer a more liquid cream texture pour it over the back of a spoon held close to the coffee's surface.

The perfect Irish coffee contains four distinct flavors and textures: hot coffee, strong whiskey, sweet sugar and cold, thick cream.

JAMAICAN COFFEE

1 ounce rum
1 ounce Tia Maria liqueur
4 ounces hot black coffee
1 teaspoon sugar or 1 sugar cube
heavy cream, whipped

Put sugar into a warm mug or heat-resistant glass, add coffee, rum and Tia Maria and stir. Float the cream on top — the more it's whipped, the easier it will be to float it. If you prefer a more liquid cream texture pour it over the back of a spoon held close to the coffee's surface.

KIOKI COFFEE

1 ounce brandy
1 ounce Kahlua liqueur
4 ounces hot black coffee
1 teaspoon sugar or 1 sugar cube
heavy cream, whipped

Put sugar into a warm mug or heat-resistant glass, add coffee, brandy and Kahlua and stir. Float the cream on top — the more it's whipped, the easier it will be to float it. If you prefer a more liquid cream texture pour it over the back of a spoon held close to the coffee's surface.

KAHLUA COFFEE

4 ounces strong black coffee
1 ounce Kahlua liqueur
whipped cream
grated orange rind

Add Kahlua to coffee, top with cream, sprinkle with grated orange rind.

NEW ORLEANS CAFE AU LAIT

6-8 cups hot strong chicory coffee
3 cups whole milk
⅓ to ½ cup heavy cream

Combine the milk and cream in a saucepan and heat just to the boil, then immediately remove from the flame. Fill six to eight large mugs one-third full of coffee, then pour in the hot milk and cream until cups are two-thirds full. Vary strength by varying proportions of milk to coffee, but always pour in the coffee first. In New Orleans cafes, waiters sometimes make a show of pouring the coffee and hot milk simultaneously in two streams that meet in air above the cups. *Makes 6-8 servings.*

ADORN COFFEE DRINKS WITH SHAVED CHOCOLATE, A DUSTING OF UNSWEETENED COCOA, A PEPPERMINT STICK, A TWIST OF ORANGE RIND, GRATED ORANGE OR LEMON RIND, A SPRINKLING OF COARSE BROWN OR NATURAL SUGAR, OR CHOCO-LATE-COVERED ROASTED COFFEE BEANS, AVAILABLE AT SPECIALTY SHOPS. YOU CAN MAKE YOUR OWN CHOCO-LATE-COVERED COFFEE BEANS BY DIPPING ESPRESSO BEANS IN MELTED CHOCO-LATE. ALLOW TO HARDEN ON WAXED PAPER.

MEXICAN COFFEE

1 ounce tequila
1 ounce Kahlua liqueur
4 ounces hot black coffee
1 teaspoon sugar or 1 sugar cube
heavy cream, whipped

Put sugar into a warm mug or heat-resistant glass, add coffee, tequila and Kahlua and stir. Float the cream on top — the more it's whipped, the easier it will be to float it. If you prefer a more liquid cream texture pour it over the back of a spoon held close to the coffee's surface.

SPECIAL COFFEE

1 ounce Grand Marnier
1 ounce Cointreau
1 ounce Tia Maria
1 ounce vodka
strong hot coffee
whipped cream
chocolate shavings

Pour liqueurs and vodka into a large brandy snifter and fill with coffee. Stir and top with whipped cream. Garnish with chocolate shavings.

VENETIAN COFFEE

2 ounches brandy
4 ounces hot black coffee
1 teaspoon sugar or 1 sugar cube
heavy cream, whipped

Put sugar into a warm mug or heat-resistant glass, add coffee and brandy and stir. Float the cream on top — the more it's whipped, the easier it will be to float it. If you prefer a more liquid cream texture pour it over the back of a spoon held close to the coffee's surface.

IF YOU ENJOY THE PAIRING OF COFFEE AND SPIRITS, TRY EMBELLISHING TRADITIONAL TREATS WITH THESE FLAVORS. USE STRONG COLD COFFEE AND RUM INSTEAD OF WATER IN A CHOCOLATE COOKIE RECIPE, PRESOAK RAISINS IN RUM WHEN MAKING RAISIN COOKIES, ADD ESPRESSO TO CHOCOLATE MOUSSE AND BRANDY AND COFFEE TO CHEESECAKE RECIPES. DESSERTS WITH CREAM OR CHOCOLATE ARE ESPECIALLY GOOD CANDIDATES FOR THE ADDITION OF COFFEE AND SPIRITS.

GIN

*J*oys of juniper . . . The preferred drink of the British, gin has enjoyed a colorful history. Gin was created in Holland by the sixteenth-century physician Dr. Sylvius, who was seeking a remedy for the tropical diseases introduced to Europe by seamen of the Dutch East India Company. The Dutch doctor redistilled grain alcohol with juniper berries, known for their medicinal properties. The concoction was named *Genievre* (the French name for juniper berry), or *genever* in Dutch. Although it proved useless as a medicine, it became immensely popular as a flavorful spirituous drink.

English soldiers discovered *genever* during the seventeenth-century wars on the Continent, and nicknamed it "Dutch courage." They brought it back to England, where its name was shortened to gin. Cheap yet palatable, gin became the tipple of choice of the London slums. Later, during Prohibition in America, the notorious "bathtub gin" was a favorite in the speakeasies.

The modern scientific making of gin has come a long way from the bathtub. Freshly made grain spirits are redistilled with juniper berries and aromatic herbs and spices. The resulting liquor is diluted with water to bring it down to the proper proof. Gin is not aged, but may be drunk fresh from the still.

The two main types of gin are London Dry and Hollands, and they are quite different in character. London Dry is the designation for both American and English gin. London Dry is based on high-proof grain spirits produced in a column still. These spirits are reduced in proof by adding distilled water, and are then redistilled in a pot still with juniper berries and other botanicals such as lemon and orange peel, anise, cassia bark, cardamom, coriander, angelica, and other ingredients, depending on the formula of the individual distiller. The herbal ingredients may either be added directly to the grain spirit before distilling, or suspended in a separate chamber known as the gin head, through which the alcoholic vapors rise. The gin is then diluted with water and ready for drinking.

London dry gin is generally can be used as a mixer or served straight over ice. The English and American varieties differ somewhat in flavor. English gin is produced at slightly lower proof, and tends to have a little more character.

Hollands gin, also known as Genever or Schiedams (after a Dutch distilling town), has a full body and a robust flavor reminiscent of malt. The spirits used in Hollands gin are made in an old-fashioned pot still from a mash high in barley malt along with other grains. It is then redistilled with juniper berries and other flavoring agents, with juniper more prominent than in London dry gin. Because they are distilled at relatively low proof, Hollands gins are full-bodied and retain a malty aroma and taste. The pronounced flavor of Hollands gin would overwhelm most mixed drinks, and so they are best taken straight and icy cold.

Gin

GIN CLASSIC

MARTINI

2½ ounces Gin
¼ ounce dry vermouth

Note: Two aspects of the classic Martini should be discussed here, ice and vermouth: there must be enough of both to make this drink properly. Fill your shaker with ice; as it is stirred or shaken, the ice dilutes the drink as well as chilling it. As for the vermouth, it is an essential ingredient, in spite of all the amusing tales of how to put in the least amount (Winston Churchill contended the best recipe involved a quick glance in the direction of an unopened bottle of vermouth while pouring the gin). See page 20 for tips on Martini-making.

Fill shaker with ice; add vermouth first, so you can pour some out if you overdo it, then the gin; stir or shake for about ten seconds, strain into chilled Martini glass. Garnish with a green olive, a twist of lemon peel, or, for the classic Gibson, a cocktail onion.

GIBSON

2½ ounces gin
½ ounce dry vermouth

Fill mixing glass with ice, add gin and vermouth, and stir to chill. Strain into a Martini glass and garnish with a cocktail onion.

GIMLET

2 ounces gin
½ ounce Rose's Lime Juice

Combine ingredients in an ice-filled shaker. Stir well and strain into a Martini glass. Garnish with wedge of fresh lime.

GIN AND TONIC

2 ounces gin
tonic water

Fill a highball glass with ice, add gin, top with tonic water. Garnish with squeeze of fresh lime.

GIN RICKEY

2 ounces gin
club soda
large wedge of fresh lime

Fill a highball glass with ice, add gin and soda, squeeze in lime and stir.

MANY NATIONS CLAIM THE MARTINI AS THEIR OWN. THE BRITISH SAY IT WAS NAMED IN HONOR OF THE BRITISH IMPERIAL ARMY'S MARTINI AND HENRY RIFLE, FAMOUS FOR ITS SPOT-ON ACCURACY. THE ITALIANS SAY IT WAS INVENTED BY THE ITALIAN VERMOUTH PRODUCERS MARTINI AND ROSSI. SAN FRANCISCANS TRACE IT TO THE FAMOUS BARTENDER JERRY THOMAS, CLAIMING THAT HE CREATED IT ON A HOT DAY IN THE MID-1800S FOR A STRANGER ENROUTE TO THE TOWN OF MARTINEZ.

BUT IN THE TOWN OF MARTINEZ, WHERE THE MARTINI FESTIVAL IS HELD EACH YEAR, CITIZENS SAY THE DRINK DATES TO THE DAYS OF THE GOLD RUSH, WHEN IT WAS CONCOCTED BY A CLEVER BARTENDER WHO HAD NO CHAMPAGNE TO OFFER A CELEBRATING MINER.

TOM COLLINS

2 ounces gin
1 ounce lemon juice
1 teaspoon superfine sugar
club soda

In a cocktail shaker, dissolve sugar in lemon juice. Add ice, gin, and soda. Shake briskly and strain over ice in a Collins glass. Top with club soda, stir; garnish with a maraschino cherry. *Note: Bottled sweet and sour mix may be substituted for the lemon juice and sugar.*

BRONX COCKTAIL, DRY

2 ounces gin
½ ounce dry vermouth
juice of ½ orange

Combine ingredients in shaker filled with ice, shake briskly, strain into chilled Martini glass.

Note: For a sweet Bronx Cocktail, reduce gin by ½ ounce and add ½ ounce sweet vermouth.

DEPTH CHARGE

1½ ounces gin
1½ ounces Lillet
2 dashes Pernod

Combine ingredients in shaker with ice cubes, shake briskly, strain into chilled Martini glass.

ELEGANT

1½ ounces gin
1½ ounces dry vermouth
2 dashes Grand Marnier

Combine ingredients in a mixing glass, stir thoroughly, strain into a chilled cocktail glass.

GIN FIZZ

3 ounces gin
1½ ounces lemon juice
1 teaspoon superfine sugar
club soda

Combine ingredients in blender with ice and mix for 10 seconds. Or put them in a cocktail shaker with crushed ice and shake briskly. Pour into a Martini glass; garnish with a lemon twist.

NEGRONI

1 ounce gin
1 ounce Campari
1 ounce sweet vermouth

Pour over ice in a rocks glass; garnish with a lemon twist.

PERFECT MARTINI

2 ounces gin
½ ounce dry vermouth
½ ounce sweet vermouth

Pour ingredients into a ice-filled mixing glass and stir well. Strain into a Martini glass.

PINK GIN

3 ounces gin
2 dashes Angostura bitters

Pour over ice in a rocks glass, stir.

WHITE LADY

2 ounces gin
1 ounce Cointreau
½ ounce lemon juice

Combine all ingredients in a shaker with ice, shake briskly, strain into a chilled Martini glass.

GIN AMERICANO

1 ounce gin
1 ounce Campari
1 ounce sweet vermouth
soda water or seltzer

Pour liquors over ice in a rocks glass; add soda and stir. Garnish with a lemon twist.

THE PUNCH BOWL

Long before the invention of mixed cocktails, the sharing of alcoholic concoctions from a communal bowl was an essential ingredient of parties and celebrations. Some claim that the word punch comes from the Hindustani *panch*, which means five, referring to the five elements thought necessary for a balanced brew — sweet, sour, strong, weak, and water. Others say it derives from the English word puncheon, the small cask from which British seamen were served their rations of rum.

Punches may be strong or weak, or non-alcoholic; they may be hot or cold; and they may be made with champagne, wine, or distilled spirits. The common element is their attractive presentation and the spirit of celebration in which they are served.

First, select the right type of punch for your party. Save the truly potent concoctions for small parties of experienced drinkers who understand moderation in the enjoyment of strong beverages. Less potent punches are appropriate for a party of mixed ages. And the considerate host will always provide a second, non-alcoholic punch equally delicious and festive.

Estimate the number of servings that you will need so that you will have right quantities of ingredients. A typical punch cup holds four ounces, and the average guest generally consumes two or three servings. One gallon of punch will therefore provide 32 servings. Some hosts consider the traditional punch cups too small, and prefer to use rocks glasses. In this case plan on an average of two servings per guest. And adjust your shopping list accordingly.

Use a punch bowl that is appropriate for the event and for the kind of punch. For a cold punch the bowl should be big enough to hold a large block of ice; for a hot punch, use a heatproof container that will allow you to serve the punch piping hot. Rent or borrow a punch bowl if you do not have the right kind.

Use only high-quality ingredients. Do not assume that because you are combining ingredients, you will be able to conceal an inferior whiskey, wine, or mixer. Squeeze fruit juices in advance from fresh ripe fruits, and strain the juice to keep the punch clear. Frozen fruits or juices are all right if fresh are not available, but avoid canned ingredients.

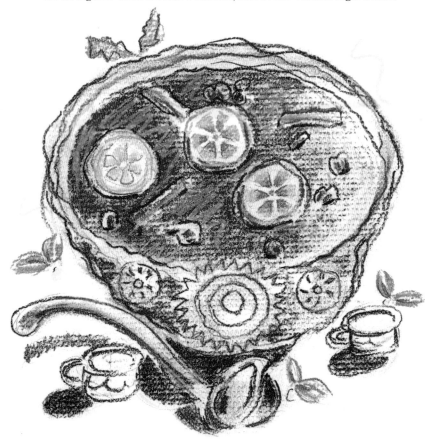

Have adequate supplies of all your ingredients so that you can refill the bowl as necessary. If you have any punch left over, it will keep in the refrigerator in a tightly sealed container for several weeks.

Allow two quarts of ice per gallon of cold punch. Use a single large block of ice; do not use ice cubes because they melt too fast. If you cannot obtain large blocks of ice, freeze your own in milk cartons, or in ice trays from which the dividers have been removed. For a champagne punch, you may wish to seat the punch bowl in a ring of ice, instead of floating ice in the bowl. Freeze water in bundt pans and pudding molds to make decorative ice rings for punches.

Chill all ingredients for a cold punch — spirits, wines, juices, fruits, and even the bowl — for one hour or so, to avoid dilution when ice is added.

Dissolve the sweetener by combining it with the juices and other non-alcoholic ingredients. Then add the alcoholic beverages about an hour before serving, and the sparkling wine and carbonated mixers just before serving. Stir gently to preserve the fizz.

If possible, chill mixed punch overnight in a tightly closed container. This allows the flavors to blend and mellow, and the sediment to settle at the bottom of the container. The punch is then poured off at serving time, leaving the sediment behind.

When it is time to refill the punch bowl, remove the bowl, empty and rinse it, and add a fresh block of ice. Prepare the new batch with the same care you did the first, chilling and mixing according to the same rules. Serve the fresh bowl of punch with clean cups. Your guests will appreciate your attention to detail.

The Punch Bowl

BARBADOS BOWL

6 bananas
1 cup lime juice
1 cup superfine sugar
12 ounces dark rum
12 ounces light rum
12 ounces mango nectar
42 ounces pineapple juice
1 orange, sliced
1 lime, sliced
⅓ fresh pineapple, sliced

Combine bananas, lime juice and sugar in an electric blender, blend until smooth. Pour into punch bowl, add rums, nectar and pineapple juice, stir well. Regrigerate until well chilled. Float an ice ring in the bowl at serving time and garnish with orange, pineapple and lime slices.

BOURBON FOG

1 liter bourbon
32 ounces strong black coffee, chilled
1 quart vanilla ice cream

In a punch bowl, stir together bourbon and coffee, spoon in ice cream and stir until creamy. Set punch bowl in a deep tray of crushed ice or seat in an ice jacket.

CHRISTMAS PUNCH

750 ml bottle brandy
750 ml chilled champagne
8 ounces superfine sugar
8 ounces cubed pineapple

Pour 2 ounces of brandy into a cup and set aside. Pour remaining brandy, champagne, sugar and pineapple into a large kettle. Stirring frequently over medium heat, bring mixture to foam, but do not boil. Remove from heat, carefully pour in reserved brandy and ignite. Wait one minute before ladling punch into cups.

CHAMPAGNE PUNCH

2 cups superfine sugar
3 ounces cognac
3 ounces maraschino
3 ounces curaçao
4 ounces lemon juice
1 liter club soda
3 bottles chilled champagne

Combine all ingredients except champagne and stir until sugar is completely dissolved. Slowly pour in champagne. Set punch bowl in a deep tray of crushed ice or seat in an ice jacket.

CLARET CUP

750 ml bottle red wine, chilled
2 ounces brandy
2 ounces Cointreau
1 tablespoon superfine sugar
16 ounces club soda, chilled
1 lemon, sliced
1 lime, sliced
⅓ fresh pineapple, sliced

Combine wine, brandy, Cointreau and sugar in a punch bowl and stir until sugar is completely dissolved, then stir in club soda. Float sliced fruit garnishes and an ice ring.

FESTIVAL PUNCH

1 liter dark Jamaican rum
32 ounces sweet apple cider
3 cinnamon sticks
2 teaspoons ground allspice
2 tablespoons butter

Combine ingredients in a large kettle. Over medium heat, bring mixture to foam, but do not boil. Serve immediately.

FISH HOUSE PUNCH

12 ounces superfine sugar
2½ quarts water
1 quart lemon juice
2 750 ml bottles dark Jamaican rum
500 ml peach brandy

Pour sugar into a punch bowl and stir in sufficient water to completely dissolve the sugar. Stir in lemon juice, rum, brandy and remaining water and refreigerate until thoroughly chilled. Float ice block immediately before serving.

GOLDEN CHAMPAGNE

¾ cup simple syrup, chilled
(see page 19 for syrup recipe)
1 cup fresh lemon juice
¾ cup Grand Marnier
1 quart sparkling water, chilled
2 bottles dry champagne, well
chilled

Combine and garnish with lemon and orange slices and strawberries. *Makes 24 four-ounce servings, or about three quarts.*

TOM AND JERRY

12 large eggs, separated and at room temperature
¼ teaspoon cream of tartar
2 cups superfine sugar
2¼ cups brandy
9 cups hot milk
Nutmeg to garnish

Beat the egg whites and cream of tartar with a whisk or electric mixer until stiff. Set aside. Beat the egg yolks and sugar with a whisk or electric mixer until thick. Fold the egg white and egg mixtures together. Put the brandy and hot milk in a warmed punch bowl and fold in the egg mixture. Ladle into mugs and garnish with freshly grated nutmeg. *Makes about 12 servings, one cup each.*

MULLED WINE

2 cups water
¾ cup sugar
Peel of one medium orange
Peel of one medium lemon
3 whole cloves
4 whole allspice berries
1 cinnamon stick, about 2 inches long
4 cups red wine, preferably Burgundy
½ cup orange juice
¼ cup crème de cassis

Bring the water, sugar, citrus peels, and spices to a simmer in a small saucepan and simmer ten minutes. Heat the wine, juice, and crème de cassis in another saucepan over moderate heat. Strain the spice mixture into the wine mixture and heat through. Pour into a warmed punch bowl and garnish with apples studded with whole cloves, citrus slices, and cinnamon sticks. Ladle into cups to serve. *Makes about eight servings of half-cup each.*

ORANGE CUP PUNCH

6 ounces chilled orange juice
16 ounces chilled white wine
liter chilled rose wine
superfine sugar
1 orange, thinly sliced

Combine wines and juice in a punch bowl. Add sugar to taste and stir until completely dissolved. Float orange slices and an ice ring.

PHI BETA BLUEBERRY

25.4-ounce bottle vodka
16 ounces Metaxa brandy
16 ounces blueberry syrup
12 ounces lemon juice
2 quarts club soda
2 lemons, sliced thin
1 pint blueberries

Pour vodka, brandy, syrup and lemon juice into punch bowl and stir. Refrigerate one hour. Float block, mold or ring of ice. Pour in club soda, garnish with lemon slices and blueberries.

PUNCH-A-CREME

6 egg yolks
2 cans evaporated milk
1 can condensed milk
½ 750 ml bottle dark Jamaican rum
2 dashes Angostura bitters
grated nutmeg

Beat egg yolks into evaporated and condensed milk. Pour mixture into punch bowl, add rum and bitters, stir well. Sprinkle with nutmeg and float an ice ring.

RUM PUNCH

1½ pounds sugar
1 quart water
750 ml bottle dark Jamaican rum
juice of 8 limes
2 dashes Angostura bitters

Boil sugar and water in a saucepan over medium heat to make a simple syrup. Cool mixture and pour into punch bowl. Add remaining ingredients and stir well. Float an ice ring.

SOCIETY HILL PUNCH

8 ounces dark Jamaican rum
2 ounces triple sec
2 ounces kirsch
2 ounces grenadine
3 tangerines, sectioned
1 grapefruit, sectioned
2 cups fresh pineapple cubes
2 750 ml bottles chilled champagne

Combine ingredients in a punch bowl, refrigerate until well chilled. Garnish with fresh mint leaves and float an ice ring.

THE WASSAIL BOWL IS A TIME-HONORED EUROPEAN TRADITION. IT TAKES ITS NAME FROM THE MIDDLE ENGLISH WORD WASSAYL, FROM AN OLD NORSE WORD MEANING "TO BE IN GOOD HEALTH." THE OLD WORLD MEETS THE NEW IN A TRADITIONAL SPANISH-INFLUENCED MEXICAN PUNCH, PONCHE NAVIDEÑO, MADE WITH WHITE WINE, RUM, TROPICAL FRUIT, SECTIONS OF SUGAR CANE, AND CINNAMON STICKS.

WASSAIL

1 pound superfine sugar
1 teaspoon grated nutmeg
1 teaspoon ginger
3 whole cloves
¼ teaspoon mace
3 whole allspice
½ teaspoon ground cinnamon
8 ounces water
6 eggs, separated
2 750 ml bottles sherry
500 ml bottle brandy

In a kettle, combine sugar, nutmeg, ginger, cloves, mace, allspice, cinnamon and water. Stir until sugar is dissolved, add sherry and simmer over low heat. Beat egg whites and yolks separately, then add to sherry mixture in kettle. Simmer 30 minutes, stirring frequently. Stir in brandy, remove from heat and serve in warmed mugs.

RUM

*L*ovely rum, romance of the Tropics. Native to the islands of the Caribbean, rum is made from sugar cane. Virtually every island produces its own rum, each with a distinctive character, ranging from the pale dry Puerto Rican white to the rich, dark rums of Jamaica. Only a few of the local rums are exported.

Rum figured prominently in the history of the colonial period. As one of the cornerstones of the notorious triangle trade, rum was manufactured in New England out of molasses from the Caribbean, and was exchanged in Africa for slaves to work the island plantations. Rum was the "grog" that was dispensed to the British navy as an unscientific precaution against scurvy, and the drink that steeled the nerves of the pirates who plied the Spanish main.

Unlike grain spirits, in which the starch must first be converted to sugar, rum is produced by directly fermenting the juice of the sugar cane or its derivative, molasses. Yeast is added to the molasses to begin the fermenting process, the fermented liquid is then distilled at relatively low proofs below 190, and the resultant spirits are aged in barrels.

In general the light rums come from the Spanish islands, while the former English colonies produce the dark rums. Light rums, exemplified by those of Puerto Rico and Cuba, as well as the Virgin Islands, are produced in patent or column stills. Fresh from the still, some white or "silver" rums resemble vodka in color and taste. On aging, light rums become golden rums; if aged at least four to six years, they can become *anejos* ("aged") or premium light rums. The mellow *anejos* are generally drunk neat or on the rocks.

Richly flavored dark rums come from Jamaica, Haiti, Barbados, Trinidad, and Martinique. They are produced in pot stills, or may be blends of pot- and column-distilled rums. Fermentation of dark rums is generally begun by adding "dunder," or skimmings from the sugar boiler, to the mash; natural air-borne yeast settles on the liquid and

multiplies, producing slow fermentation. Dark rums are generally aged in casks longer than light rums, and caramel is added to enhance the color. The dark and potent Demerara rums of Guyana can run as high as 151 proof, and should be approached with appropriate respect.

Rum is traditionally drunk straight on its islands of origin. In this country it is commonly mixed in cocktails, including popular fruit drinks such as the Daiquiri.

Rum

THE CLASSICS

CUBA LIBRÉ

1½ ounces golden rum
large wedge of fresh lime
cola

Fill highball glass with ice, add rum and cola to fill; squeeze lime into glass and stir.

DAIQUIRI

2 ounces white or golden rum
juice of lime half
1 teaspoon superfine sugar
Briskly shake ingredients in an ice-filled shaker; strain into a cocktail glass.

Frozen Daiquiris have a wonderful texture. Pour the ingredients over a heaping cup of crushed ice in an electric blender, blend until smooth and foamy, and pour into a chilled wine glass.

FROZEN FRUIT DAIQUIRIS

Add ½ cup sliced strawberries (or another fruit such as bananas or peaches) to your Daiquiris before blending. Would be more delicious for a brunch party?

MAI TAI

2 ounces dark or medium rum
1 ounce Rose's Lime Juice
3 dashes orgeat syrup
¾ ounce orange curaçao

Briskly shake ingredients with four ice cubes in a cocktail shaker, strain over fresh ice in a highball glass.

PINA COLADA

2 ounces golden rum
3 ounces crushed pineapple or unsweetened pineapple juice
1½ ounce cream of coconut

Pour ingredients into an electric blender filled with a heaping cup of crushed ice, blend until smooth. Pour into rocks glass or over ice in a wine goblet or Collins glass.

RUM AND TONIC

1½ ounces golden rum
ice cold tonic water

Pour rum over ice in a highball glass, top off with tonic, garnish with a lime wedge.

APPLE PIE

1½ ounces light rum
1½ ounces sweet vermouth
4 dashes apricot brandy
4 dashes lemon juice
2 dashes grenadine

Briskly shake ingredients with four ice cubes in a cocktail shaker, strain over fresh ice in a highball glass.

BACARDI COCKTAIL

3 ounces light Bacardi rum
juice of fresh lime half
2 dashes grenadine

Briskly shake ingredients with four ice cubes in a cocktail shaker, strain over fresh ice in a highball glass.

BAHIA

1 ounce light rum
1 ounce golden rum
1 ounces coconut cream
2 ounces pineapple juice

Briskly shake ingredients with four ice cubes in a cocktail shaker, strain over fresh ice in a Collins glass.

BEACHCOMBER

3 ounces light rum
1½ ounce Cointreau
juice of fresh lime half
2 dashes maraschino or grenadine

Briskly shake ingredients with four ice cubes in a cocktail shaker, strain over fresh ice in a chilled wine glass.

BEE'S KISS

2 ounces golden rum
1 teaspoon honey
1 teaspoon cream or milk

Briskly shake ingredients with ice in a cocktail shaker, strain over fresh ice in a rocks glass.

BLACK AND GOLD

1½ ounce golden rum
1½ ounce coffee liqueur
½ teaspoon instant coffee
½ teaspoon superfine sugar.

Combine ingredients with ice in a mixing glass, stir thoroughly, strain over fresh ice in a wine glass.

COUNTRY LIFE

1 ounce dark rum
1 ounce port
1½ ounce bourbon
3 dashes Angostura bitters
1 dash orange bitters

Briskly shake ingredients with ice in a cocktail shaker, strain over fresh ice in a highball glass.

HARRY'S SPECIAL

1 ounce dark rum
1 ounce light rum
1 ounce pineapple juice
2 ounces orange juice

Combine ingredients with ice in a mixing glass, stir thoroughly, strain over fresh ice in a highball glass.

HAVANA CLUB

1½ ounce golden rum
1 ounce dry vermouth

Combine ingredients with ice in a mixing glass, stir thoroughly, strain into a Martini glass.

MARY PICKFORD

1½ ounces light rum
1½ ounces pineapple juice
1 dash kirsch
1 dash grenadine

Briskly shake ingredients with ice in a cocktail shaker; strain over fresh ice in a rocks glass.

PLANTER'S PUNCH

3 ounces dark rum
1 ounce lime juice
1 tablespoon superfine sugar
1 dash curacao
1 dash Angostura bitters
club soda or seltzer

Pour ingredients over ice in a highball glass, stir lightly.

RUM AND BITTERS

3 ounces light rum
3 ounces water
½ teaspoon superfine sugar
2 dashes Angostura bitters

Pour ingredients over ice in an Old Fashioned glass, stir well.

RUM COW

1½ ounces dark rum
1 dash vanilla extract
1 pinch grated nutmeg
1 dash Angostura bitters
2 teaspoons superfine sugar
4 ounces milk

Briskly shake ingredients with four ice cubes in a cocktail shaker, strain over fresh ice in a Collins glass.

RUM DANDY

1½ ounces dark rum
2 ounces pineapple juice
1 ounce orange juice
1 teaspoon banana liqueur
1 teaspoon lime juice

Pour ingredients over a heaping cup of crushed ice in an electric blender, blend until smooth, pour into a chilled wine glass.

RUM SURPRISE

3 ounces light rum
1 teaspoon superfine sugar
grapefruit juice

Combine rum and sugar in a highball glass, pack with crushed ice and place glass in the freezer for a minimum of 15 minutes. Remove from freezer, top off with grapefruit juice and serve immediately.

SCORPION

3 ounces light rum
1½ ounces brandy
2 ounces lemon juice
3 ounces orange juice
1 ounce orgeat syrup

Pour ingredients over a heaping cup of crushed ice in an electric blender, blend until smooth, pour into a chilled Collins or wine glass.

SHANGHAI

1½ ounces dark rum
½ ounce lemon juice
1 ounce Sambuca
1 dash grenadine

Briskly shake ingredients with ice in a cocktail shaker; strain into a cocktail glass.

SHARK'S TOOTH

1½ ounces light rum
1 ounce rum
1 ounce lemon juice
1 ounce lime juice
½ teaspoon superfine sugar
1 dash grenadine
club soda or seltzer

Combine rum, lemon juice, lime juice, sugar and grenadine with ice in a mixing glass and stir briskly and thoroughly. Strain into a Collins glass over fresh ice and top off with club soda.

SUNBURN

1½ ounces light rum
½ ounce Cointreau
½ ounce lime juice
3 dashes Amaretto

Briskly shake ingredients with four ice cubes in a cocktail shaker, strain over fresh ice in a rocks glass.

ZOMBIE

1 ounce dark rum
1 ounce golden rum
1 ounce light rum
1 ounce pineapple juice
1 ounce papaya juice, optional
juice of fresh lime half
1 teaspoon superfine sugar

Briskly shake ingredients with four ice cubes in a cocktail shaker, strain over fresh ice in a Collins glass.

Making a Rumtopf

Spirits are a perfect medium for preserving fruit. The traditional European *rumtopf* (German for rum pot) is a crock of fresh fruit layered as each comes into season and steeped in sweetened rum or brandy. The fruit is delicious alone, or served over ice cream or cake, or with whipped cream or sour cream over pancakes or Belgian waffles.

To make a *rumtopf*, prepare a large clean glass or ceramic crock with a lid by washing well with very hot water. As each fruit comes in season, seed, stem and pit the fruit and sprinkle with ½ cup sugar to each pound of fruit. Let the fruit stand overnight. Then add it gently to the rumptof, being careful not to disturb the layer of fruit beneath it. Pour in rum or brandy to cover. Replace the lid and store in a cool, dry place. Allow the fruit to mature for a few weeks after each addition of fruit. Most ripe, perfect fruit can be used, but the best choices are strawberries, sour cherries, apricots, peaaches, plum, pears and pineapple.

Spirit-steeped fruits will keep almost indefinitely.

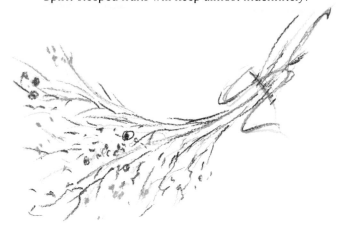

TEQUILA

*T*equila is the spirit of the desert. Locked in the heart of the agave, or maguey, the great spiked plant of the Mexican desert, is a juice known as *aguamiel*, or "honey water." When it ferments, this juice becomes *pulque*, probably the first alcoholic beverage native to the New World. Pulque is drunk freshly made, close to its place of origin. When the Spanish conquerors introduced the art of distillation, the same maguey juice was used to produce distilled spirits. Of the more than 400 varieties of the agave plant, only one, the blue agave, is used to make tequila. The plants are cultivated in a small, government-defined area around the town of the same name in the state of Jalisco.

Once considered little more than a curiosity in American bars, tequila has recently enjoyed a meteoric rise in popularity. Its pungent taste forms the basis for an endless variety of mixed drinks incorporating other spirits, liqueurs, and fruit juices.

Tequila's reputation for a harsh taste and potent punch is probably based on confusion with other, cruder spirits, derived from other varieties of agave. These include mescal, as well as a number of locally produced and consumed forms of moonshine. True tequila is generally produced at 80 to 86 proof, similar to the other popular spirits.

The distillers around the town of Tequila harvest the huge maguey plants after a twelve-year growing period. The hearts are steam cooked and shredded, the juice is pressed out, and the resultant mash fermented with sugar. The liquid is then double distilled in pot stills to bring the alcoholic content up to just over 100 proof. White tequila fresh from the still has a raw, fiery taste, and is used in mixed drinks. When aged in oak, it takes on a golden color and acquires a smoother, mellower taste. After at least four years it can be marketed as *tequila anejo*. The older *anejos* are worthy of sipping straight, without dilution. Many tequilas exported to the United States are made of a blend of agave and sugar cane, and have a lighter flavor.

Tequila

T H E C L A S S I C S

TEQUILA SUNRISE

1½ ounces tequila
orange juice
½ ounce grenadine

Fill a Collins glass with ice, add tequila, fill with orange juice and top with grenadine. Stir. Garnish with a lime and a cherry. Slowly pour grenadine on the top so that it trickles down the drink, creating the sunrise effect.

MARGARITA

2 ounces tequila
½ ounce Cointreau or
    Triple Sec
½ ounce sweet and sour mix
or ¼ ounce lime juice

Coat the rim of a sauce cocktail glass or wine glass by moistening with lime juice (run a lime wedge around the rim), then turning it upside down in a saucer of coarse salt.

Put glass in the freezer while preparing drink. Combine ingredients in a cocktail shaker with lots of ice and shake briskly — or, for a better texture, use an electric blender. Strain into a chilled glass and garnish with a wedge of lime.

ACAPULCO

1½ ounces tequila
1½ ounces dark rum
3 ounces pinapple juice
1 ounce grapefruit juice

Combine ingredients in an ice-filled cocktail shaker, shake briskly, strain over fresh ice in a Collins glass.

TEQUILA GRAPE

1½ ounces tequila
juice of fresh lime half
1 dash grenadine
grapefruit juice

Combine tequila, lime juice and grenadine in an ice-filled shaker, shake briskly, strain over fresh ice in a highball glass, top with grapefruit juice.

TEQUILA COLLINS

1½ ounces tequila
1-2 ounces lemon juice
1 teaspoon superfine sugar
club soda or seltzer

Combine lemon juice and sugar in a Collins glass and stir to dissolve; add tequila and ice, and fill with soda. Garnish with a cherry or an orange slice. *Note: Bottled sweet and sour mix may be substituted for the lemon juice and sugar.*

BLACK BULL

2 ounces tequila
1 ounce coffee liqueur

Fill a rocks glass with ice, add tequila and coffee liqueur, stir.

BLOODY MARIA

1½ ounces tequila
4 dashes worcestershire sauce
2 dashes Tabasco
1 pinch fresh horseradish
Salt and pepper to taste
4 ounces tomato juice

Briskly shake ingredients with four ice cubes in a cocktail shaker, strain over fresh ice in a Collins glass. Garnish with a celery stalk.

BLOODY BULL

2 ounce tequila
1 ounce lemon juice
1 dash worcestershire sauce
1 dash Tabasco
2 ounce beef bouillon
2 ounces tomato juice

Combine tequila, lemon juice, worchestershire sauce and Tabasco with ice a cocktail shaker, shake well, strain over fresh ice in a Collins glass. Add bouillon and tomato juice, stir lightly and garnish with a wedge of fresh lime.

SOMBRERO

1½ ounces tequila
1½ ounces coffee liqueur
1 ounce half and half

Pour tequila and coffee liqueur over ice in a rocks glass, add cream and stir.

CHARRO

1½ ounces tequila
1½ ounces evaporated milk
1 ounce cold black coffee

Combine ingredients with ice in a cocktail shaker, shake briskly, strain over fresh ice in a rocks glass.

EL DIABLO

1½ ounces tequila
juice of fresh lime half
1 ounce crème de cassis
ginger ale

Fill a highball glass with ice, add tequila, lime juice and crème de cassis, top with ginger ale.

EVITA

3 ounces tequila
bitter lemon

Fill a highball glass with crushed ice, add tequila, place in freezer for a minimum of ten minutes. Remove from freezer, top off with bitter lemon.

HAND GRENADE

1½ ounces tequila
3 ounces cranberry juice

Combine ingredients with ice in a mixing glass, stir thoroughly, strain over fresh ice in a rocks glass. Garnish with an orange twist.

MEXICAN LOVER

2 ounces tequila
1 ounce brandy
1 ounce sweet vermouth

Combine ingredients with ice in a mixing glass, stir thoroughly, strain over fresh ice in a highball glass.

MEXITINI

2½ ounces tequila
½ ounce dry vermouth

Combine ingredients with ice in a mixing galss, stir thoroughly, strain into a Martini glass.

TEQUILA GIVES A SUCCULENT TWIST TO OLD FAVORITES. TRY IT IN PLACE OF WINE OR VINEGAR IN MARINADES FOR MEATS YOU ARE PLANNING TO GRILL, OR IN SAUCES INSTEAD OF WINE.

TEQUILA ESPAÑA

1½ ounces tequila
1½ ounces medium sherry

Fill a wine glass with ice, add tequila and sherry, stir very lightly.

TEQUILA MANHATTAN

2 ounces tequila
½ ounce sweet vermouth
1 dash orange bitters

Combine ingredients with ice in a mixing glass, stir thoroughly, strain into a cocktail glass or over ice in a rocks glass. Garnish with a lemon twist.

TEQUILA SUNSET

1½ ounces tequila
3 to 4 ounces orange juice
½ ounce blackberry brandy

Fill a highball glass with ice, add tequila, fill with orange juice. Float brandy on top by pouring slowly over the convex surface of a spoon held just abover the drink surface.

TROPICAL NIGHT

1½ ounces tequila
½ ounce grenadine
1 teaspoon lemon juice
3 ounces orange juice

Fill highball glass with ice, add ingredients, stir very lightly and garnish with an orange slice.

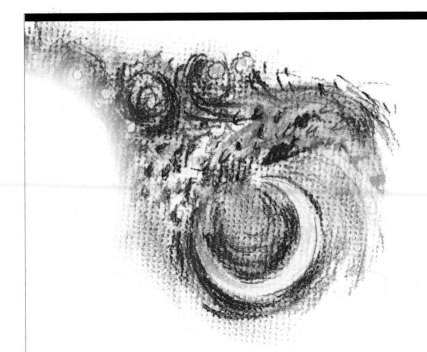

VODKA

h, vodka, the "Little Water."

Six hundred years ago, Eastern Europeans undoubtedly meant to show affecttion for their newfound drink when they named it *vodka*, a diminutive meaning "little water."

Both Poles and Russians vigorously lay claim to being the originators of vodka, back in the fourteenth century. Regardless of who first conceived the idea, it didn't take long for the rest of the Slavs to grow passionate for vodka. It was immediately popular and widely produced from almost every abundant crop in the region, including wheat, rye, maize, sugar beets, and potatoes.

In the early 1800s, the Russians invented a technique for filtering vodka through charcoal. The process lifted vodka to an undisputed plateau of purity with a smooth, crisp, and clean taste. Vodka distilleries popped up like dandelions, some offering distinctive filtering processes

using materials such as quartz sand and maple tree charcoal. At one time in Russia there was a choice of over 4,000 labels.

The rest of the world was slow to discover vodka. But suddenly in 1945, a blend of vodka, half a lime, and ginger beer served in a copper mug and called The Moscow Mule, was an overnight smash, and vodka was established in America. A Moscow Mule is a rather isolated call today, but the Screwdriver, Bloody Mary, Vodka Martini and Vodka Tonic have become veritable institutions of mixology.

Vodka is now the best-selling distilled spirit in this country, thanks to its eloquent purity when drunk straight and the unobtrusive canvas it allows mixed drinks. As a "neutral spirit," by U.S. federal regulations vodka must be "without distinctive character, aroma or taste."

Certainly, there are those who would argue hard and long that vodkas do indeed have distinctive characteristics and who are quite willing to pay for premium brands.

Since vodka is relatively free of congeners (impurities), esters and botanicals, it is often the choice of persons particularly susceptible to hangovers, headaches or allergic reactions. One vodka on the market, Skyy Vodka, even goes a step further, distilling vodka four times to assure all impurities and toxins are removed, a refinement especially appreciated by the environmentally conscious generation that made pure designer waters popular.

Vodka

THE CLASSICS

BLACK RUSSIAN

2 ounces vodka
1 ounce coffee liqueur

Pour ingredients over ice in a rocks glass; stir well. *Note: For the delicious variation called a White Russian, add one ounce of half-and-half.*

BLOODY MARY

1½ ounces vodka
3½ ounces tomato juice
½ ounce lime juice
4 dashes Worcestershire
2 dashes Tabasco
1 pinch fresh horseradish
2 dashes salt
3 dashes fresh ground pepper

Pour ingredients in a shaker with ice and shake briskly. Strain over fresh ice into a highball or Collins glass and garnish with a small stalk of celery. If recipe is too hot, adjust Tabasco and horseradish to taste.

BULLSHOT

1½ ounces vodka
4 ounces beef bouillon (cold)
1 dash Worchestershire
1 dash A-1 Sauce
1 dash Tabasco
1 dash Angostura bitters

Combine ingredients in a mixing glass and stir evenly. Strain over fresh ice cubes into a highball glass and garnish with a lemon wedge.

SCREWDRIVER

1½ ounces vodka
4 ounces orange juice

Pour vodka and juice over ice in a highball glass and stir.

BEER BUSTER

1½ ounces vodka
beer

Pour vodka into a pilsner glass and slowly top with beer.

CHANTILLY COFFEE

1 ounce vodka
1 ounce coffee schnapps
3 ounces cream
½ ounce Triple Sec

Whirl cracked ice and all ingredients in a blender until smooth or shake and strain into a wine goblet or brandy snifter.

CAPE COD

1½ ounces vodka
3 ounces cranberry juice
splash of lime juice

Fill a highball or Collins glass with ice and add ingredients.

COOCH BEHAR

Named for an Indian maharajah
1½ ounces pepper vodka
3 ounces tomato juice

Pour ingredients over ice in an old-fashioned glass.

COSMOPOLITAN

2 ounces vodka
¼ ounce cranberry juice
¼ ounce Cointreau or triple sec
¼ ounce Rose's Lime Juice

Pour all ingredients into an ice-filled mixing glass. Stir well and strain into a Martini glass.

EL PRADO

1½ ounces vodka
¾ ounce Cherry Heering
juice of one-half lime

Shake ingredients with cracked ice and strain into a champagne tulip. Twist a lime zest close to liquid and drop in.

FAN-TAN

1 ounce vodka
½ ounce rum
1 ounce coffee liqueur
2 ounces milk or cream

Combine ingredients with ice in a mixing glass and stir evenly. Strain into a highball glass over fresh rocks.

FLYING GRASSHOPPER

1½ ounces vodka
½ ounce white crème de menthe
½ ounce green crème de menthe

Shake ingredients with cracked ice in a cocktail shaker and strain into an Old Fashioned glass.

FUZZY NAVEL

1 ounce vodka
½ ounce peach schnapps
6 ounces orange juice

Shake all ingredients wtih cracked ice and strain over fresh ice in an Old Fashioned glass or whirl in a blender until smooth.

GORKI PARK

2½ ounces vodka
3 fresh strawberries
1 teaspoon grenadine
1 dash orange bitters

Place ingredients in blender with four cubes of ice and whirl at medium speed for five to ten seconds. Pour into a Martini glass and garnish with a fresh strawberrry.

GRAPE VODKA FROTH

3 ounces vodka
8 ounces grape juice
Juice of one-half lemon
1 egg white

Pour all ingredients into blender with one cup of cracked ice and whirl at high speed until smooth, about one and a half minutes Pour into Martini glasses and garnish with lemon slices.
Note: Makes four drinks.

GREEN DRAGON

1½ ounces vodka
½ ounce green crème de menthe or Chartuese

Fill a rocks glass with ice and pour vodka, then crème de menthe. Garnish with a sprig of mint.

HARVEY WALLBANGER

1½ounces vodka
4 ounces orange juice
1/2 ounce Galliano

Fill a frosted Collins glass with several ice cubes. Pour vodka and juice and stir well. Carefully float the Galliano by holding a spoon close to the liquid and slowly pouring the liqueur over the convex surface.

ICEBERG

2 ounces vodka
1 teaspoon Pernod

Shake ingredients with four cubes of ice and strain into a rocks glass over fresh ice.

JOHNNY VODKA

2 ounces vodka
Cold apple juice

Fill highball glass with ice, add vodka and top with ice cold apple juice.

KAMIKAZI

2 ounces vodka
¼ ounce Cointreau or triple sec
¼ ounce Rose's Lime Juice

Pour all ingredients into an ice-filled mixing glass. Stir well and strain into a Martini glass.

KENDALL'S FIZZ

1½ ounces vodka
½ ounce amaretto
1 ounce orange juice
1 ounce heavy cream
1 tablespoon sugar

Blend all ingredients with cracked ice in blender. Serve in a wine goblet or brandy snifter.

LONG ISLAND ICED TEA

½ ounce vodka
½ ounce white rum
½ ounce gin
½ ounce white tequila
½ ounce Triple Sec
2 ounces lemon juice
1 teaspoon superfine sugar
cola

Pour all ingredients except cola into a shaker with ice and shake gently. Strain into a Collins glass over fresh ice and fill with cola. Stir and garnish with a wedge of lemon.

Frozen variation: Omit Triple Sec, lemon juice and sugar from above recipe and substitute 3 ounces of sweet and sour mix and ¼ ounce white crème de menthe. Whirl all ingredients except cola in blender with cracked ice. Pour into glass, add cola and stir gently.

MOSCOW MULE

1½ ounces vodka
½ ounce lime juice
ginger beer or ginger ale

Fill a Collins glass with ice, add vodka and juice and top with ginger beer or ale. Garnish with a lime wedge.

NINOTCHKA

2 ounces vodka
1 teaspoon lemon juice
3 teaspoons white crème de cacao

Combine all ingredients with ice in a cocktail shaker, shake briskly and strain into a Martini glass.

POLYNESIAN PEPPER POT

A spicy hot drink
1½ ounces vodka
¾ ounces gold rum
4 ounces pineapple juice
½ ounce sugar syrup
½ teaspoon lemon juice
1 tablespoon cream
Tabasco sauce, to taste
¼ teaspoon cayenne pepper, or to taste
curry powder, to taste

Mix all ingredients except curry with cracked ice in blender or shaker. Strain into a chilled brandy snifter or a large Old Fashioned glass. Garnish with a sprinkling of curry powder.

PRAIRIE OYSTER

2 ounces vodka
1 raw egg
1 teaspoon Worcestershire
1 teaspoon catsup
½ teaspoon vinegar
1 dash salt
1 dash pepper
1 dash Tabasco
2 cubes of ice

Combine all ingredients in blender and whirl at medium speed until blended. Serve in a wine glass.

RED LIPS

1 ounce vodka
1 ounce Campari
4 ounces grapefruit juice
splash of club soda

Pour first three ingredients in the order listed into an ice-filled Collins glass. Top with a splash of soda and garnish with a mint sprig.

THE RITZ

2½ ounces vodka
¼ ounce vermouth
dash of Chartreuse

Pour Chartreuse into a Martini glass. Pour vodka and vermouth into mixing glass with ice and stir well. Strain into the glass with Chartreuse and garnish with a green grape.

THE FIRST BLOODY MARY WAS MIXED IN 1924 AT HARRY'S BAR IN PARIS BY A BARTENDER NAMED FERNAND PETIOT. HARRY'S WAS MUCH FREQUENTED BY THE AMERICAN EXPATRIOT LITERATI WHO TOOK UP RESIDENCE IN PARIS'S LEFT BANK DURING THE 1920S. THE DRINK WAS PROBABLY NAMED AFTER MARY TUDOR, THE ROMAN CATHOLIC DAUGHTER OF HENRY VIII, WHO WAS KNOWN AS BLOODY MARY DUE TO HER PENCHANT FOR EXECUTING PROTESTANT SUBJECTS IN ORDER TO SAVE THEIR SOULS.

RUBINO

1½ ounce vodka
1 ounce red Dubonnet
½ ounce Campari

Combine all ingredients in a mixing glass and ice and stir evenly. Strain into a rocks glass over fresh ice and garnish with a cherry.

RUSSIAN NAIL

1½ ounce vodka
½ ounce Drambuie

Fill a rocks glass with ice, add ingredients and garnish with a lemon twist.

SALTY DOG

2 ounces vodka
4 ounces grapefruit juice

Salt the rim of a Collins or highball glass and fill with ice cubes. Add vodka and juice and garnish with a wedge of lime.

SEABREEZE

1½ ounces vodka
2 ounces grapefruit juice
3 ounces cranberry juice

Combine ingredients in mixing glass with ice. Stir evenly and strain into a highball glass over fresh ice.

SEX ON THE BEACH

2 ounces vodka
1 ounce peach schnapps
3-4 ounces pineapple juice
1 ounce crème de cassis

Shake with cracked ice and strain into a rocks glass.

STRAW HAT

1 ounce vodka
2 ounces Malibu or CocoRibe
6 strawberries

Place all ingredients except one strawberry in a blender along with cracked ice. Whirl until smooth and pour into a frosted wine goblet. Garnish with a strawberry.

TWISTER

2 ounces vodka
juice of half a fresh lime
7-Up

Fill a Collins or highball glass with ice and add vodka. Squeeze the lime half and drop in. Fill rest of glass with 7-Up.

VODKA GIBSON

2½ ounces vodka
½ ounce dry vermouth

Fill mixing glass with ice, add vermouth and vodka, and stir to chill. Strain into martini glass and garnish with a cocktail onion.

VODKA GIMLET

2 ounces vodka
½ ounce Rose's Lime Juice

Combine ingredients with ice in a mixing glass and stir evenly. Strain into a Martini glass and garnish with a lime wedge.

VODKA MARTINI

2½ ounces vodka
½ ounce dry vermouth

Fill mixing glass with ice, add vermouth and vodka, and stir to chill. Strain into a Martini glass and garnish with an olive or a lemon twist.

VODKA AND TONIC

1½ ounces vodka
cold tonic water

Fill highball glass with ice and add vodka. Fill glass with tonic and garnish with a lime wedge.

VODKA SOUR

2½ ounces vodka
2 tablespoons lemon juice
1 teaspoon superfine sugar

Combine ingredients in a cocktail shaker with ice and shake briskly. Strain into a rocks glass and garnish with a slice of orange and a maraschino cherry.

VODKA STINGER

2 ounces vodka
½ ounce white crème de menthe

Stir ingredients with ice in a mixing glass. Strain into a frosted Martini glass.

VOLGA BOATMAN

1½ ounces vodka
1½ ounces cherry brandy
1½ ounces orange juice

Combine ingredients in a mixing glass with four ice cubes and stir evenly. Strain into a Collins glass over fresh ice and garnish with a cherry.

WHITE RUSSIAN

2 ounces vodka
1 ounce coffee liqueur
1 ounce half-and-half

Pour ingredients over ice in an Old Fashioned glass. Stir well.

THE ALGONQUIN'S HOT BULL SHOT

1½ ounce vodka
6 ounces beef boullion
2 dashes Worcestershire sauce
1 to 2 dashes Tabasco
Fresh ground pepper
Lemon slice

Pour vodka and boullion into a warmed eight8-ounce mug. Spice with Worcestershire sauce, Tabasco and ground pepper. Garnish with thin slice of lemon and serve steaming hot.

SONIC TONIC

1¼ ounce vodka
6 ounces soda
H ounce tonic

Fill a 12-ounce highball glass with ice. Add chilled vodka, soda and tonic and stir. Garnish with a slice of lime.

RED SQUARE

1 ounce fresh orange juice
1 ounce fresh papaya juice
1 ounce fresh pineapple juice
1½ ounce vodka
½ ounce grenadine

Pour ingredients into a blender with plenty of cracked ice. Blend until smooth and serve in a chilled wine goblet.

Drinks with Flavored Vodkas

CITRUS CREAM

1 ½ ounce citrus-flavored vodka, ¼ ounce kirsch, 1 ounce lime juice, ½ teaspoon sugar syrup, 1 ounce light cream, slice of lime. Shake all ingredients in a shaker with ice and strain. Pour into a chilled wine goblet over fresh ice and garnish with slice of lime.

RED HOT MARTINI

3 ounces pepper-flavored vodka, dash of pepper schapps. Shake together in cocktail shaker with ice, then strain into Martini glass.

YELLOW FEVER

1 ½ ounces lemon vodka, 1 - 2 dashes lemon, lime or sugar syrup or ¼ teaspoon sugar, selter water, raspberries. Pour sugar, then vodka over ice in a rocks glass and stir. Add setzer and stir again. Garnish with fruit.

PINE MINT

1 ½ ounces mint-flavored vodka, 4 ounces pineapple juice, half slice of pineapple. Shake vodka and juice with ice in a cocktail shaker. Strain into a highball glass over fresh ice. Garnish with pineapple slice.

HERBED BLOODY MARY

1 ½ ounces herb-flavored vodka (made with thyme or basil), 4 ounces tomato juice, 2 tablespoons lime juice, pinch of salt, freshly ground black pepper, dash of Tabasco. Shake ingredients in cocktail shaker with ice. Pour over fresh ice in an Old Fashioned glass and garnish with sprig of fresh herb and thin slice of lime.

LIQUOR LEXICON

Ale *See Beer.* Generic term for English-style top-fermented beers. Bitter ale, the national drink of England, is full-bodied and malty, with higher hops content. Pale ale is the bottled equivalent of bitter ale.

Amaretto Almond-flavored liqueur.

Anisette Licorice-flavored liqueur.

Angostura bitters *See Bitters.*

Aperitif A drink intended to whet the appetite. Dry cocktails, dry sherry, but particularly patent vermouths such as Byrrh, Campari, Dubonnet, Fernet, Lillet, Punt e Mes.

Aquavit Neutral spirits flavored with caraway seed, the schnapps of Scandinavia, best drunk especially cold. A bottle of Danish Aalborg aquavit, encased in a block of ice, is a brave sight. Serve aquavit in a chilled shot glass.

B&B Brandy and Benedictine liqueur, blended and bottled.

Beer *See also Ale, Stout, Porter, Bock, Weisse bier, Malt liquor.* The beverage produced by fermenting a grain mash. Originating in Mesopotamia and Egypt more than 5,000 years ago, beer has been made by almost every world culture. The basic process of the brewer's art has changed little since Medieval times. Barley grains are germinated, dried, and roasted, thus creating malt. The malt is mixed with hot water and "cooked" into a porridge-like mush called mash. The mash is filtered and clarified to make the basic raw material for beer, called wort. The wort is boiled and hops are added to it for flavor. The hopped wort is cooled and transferred to a vessel where it is blended with yeast to encourage fermentation. Hops and yeast are not actually ingredients of beer; instead they are agents of flavoring and preservation and their influence on the resulting concoction is mysterious and delicate. The true ingredients of beer are simply barley-malt and water.

Beer styles fall into two categories related to the method of fermentation: bottom-fermented and top-fermented brews. Bottom-fermented beer, first mentioned in 1420, derives from the discovery that when beer was left to ferment in naturally cold caves (later caves chilled with natural ice, and, later still, mechanically refrigerated areas) the yeast gradually settled to the bottom of the beer and the beer did not go sour — a danger in the early days. This primary fermentation of a week or two is followed by a slow secondary fermentation of up to several months in which the last stubborn sugars yield to the yeast and the beer matures and mellows. The secondary fermentation is called *lagering* (meaning "storing"), hence the name lager beer. Top-fermented beers such as ale undergo a week-long first fermentation, then a short maturing of only a few days at the brewery. Then they are primed with sugar and sealed into casks where they build up natural carbonation as they undergo their second fermentation.

Benedictine Cognac-based liqueur.

Bitter Lemon A carbonated, non-alcoholic beverage similar to citrus-flavored tonic, drunk alone as a liquid refreshment or used as an ingredient in mixed drinks.

Bitters A generic term for bitter essences compounded from herbs and roots, fruits and flowers, prepared in alcohol and used to flavor drinks. In drink recipes, when nothing further is specified, Angostura bitters is intended.

Blended whiskey Three types: American whiskey, made by blending aged whiskey, corn and rye, generally, with grain neutral spirits; Canadian, similar to American, but lighter, perhaps more delicate, usually made with some amount of barley in the mash; Blended Scotch whiskey, pot-still malt whiskeys blended with

continuous-still malt whiskeys.

Bock *See Beer*. Strong, bottom-fermented German beer.

Bourbon American whiskey distilled from a mash of at least 51% corn, and aged in new charred white oak barrels for at least one year, but usually a good deal longer. It is named after Bourbon County, Kentucky, where it originated at the end of the 18th Century, but doesn't have to be made there to use the name. Proof ranges from 80 to 101.

Bordeaux Red wines—called claret by the English—and white wines produced near this city of southwest France and sold in distinctive shouldered bottles, celebrated worldwide.

Brandy, flavored Sweetened, flavored, brandy-based liqueurs.

Brandy Distilled fruit wine. The word is derived from burned wine, *brent vin, brenntwein, brandywine,* an apt description for the process of heating wine, then cooling (con-densing) the alcoholic vapors, thus capturing its essential spirits. The eau-de-vies of France and Switzer-land and from various fruits: plums, pears, cherries, are brandies, but if no fruit is specified, grape wine is understood to be the base. Cognac and Armagnac, beloved of the connoisseurs, are aged grape brandies from delimited areas of Frances; Martell, Remy-Martin, Hennesy, Courvoisier, Hine, and

Biscuit are respected producers of Cognac; Calvados, also prized, is apple brandy from a district in Normandy and slivovitz is plum brandy from Yugoslavia. Brandies are also produced in Spain, Germany, and California.

Burgundy In east-central France, along a string of hills stretching north and south from the city of Dijon, parallel to National Highway 74, lie the great vineyards of Burgundy. Some are tiny, two or three acres of vines. Here are produced flinty Chablis, splendid Montrachet and Meursault. Magnificent reds, too, of the Côte d'Or, the Côte de Nuits, the Côte de Beaune: Nuits St Georges, Echezeaux, Romanee-Conti, Chambertin and Gevrey Chambertin, Richebourg, Pommard. From the southern end of the area come Maçon and Beaujolais, lighter and fruitier.

Calvados *See Brandy.* Apple brandy.

Campari A patent aperitif with a complex quinine-like, refreshing taste.

Canadian Whisky of considerable lightness, distilled from rye, corn, and barley, principally, blended with neutral spirits, and aged at least three years.

Champagne Reims and Epernay, about 100 miles northeast of Paris, are the center of production of Champagne, that most spectacular of wines, the lovers' choice, the proper accompaniment to celebrations. The contribution of the legendary cellarmaster, Dom Pierre Perignon, some three centuries ago, was to induce a second fermentation in the bottle by slipping in sugar and yeast, and trapping the carbon dioxide bubbles with a tight cork held in by a clamp. When the wine has matured, the bottles are turned and tilted over a period of time to bring the sediment to the cork. Then, the neck of the bottle is frozen; the cork, released from its clamp, pops out with the sediment clinging to it. The final steps are to adjust the sweetness of the wine by quickly introducing a bit of champagne and sugar syrup (dosage), recorking, affixing the wire cage over the cork. Champagne sweetness ranges from brut (driest) to extra dry, demi sec, sec — - which is quite sweet — and doux.

Chartreuse Spicy, aromatic liqueur, either yellow or more commonly green (the origin of the name for that particular shade of yellow-green). Known for its high alcohol content, at 110%, a little goes a long way.

Chateauneuf-du-Pape Full-bodied red wine of the Rhode Valley in Provence, near Avignon, which was the papal residence in the 14th Century. Translation: The Pope's new castle.

Cherry Heering   Cherry liqueur produced in Denmark.

Chianti   Red wine made in a delimited area of Tuscany.

Club Soda   Unflavored, unsweetened carbonated water.

Cocktail   Cocktails originated in America in the 1800s. The word itself is of unknown origin, though many ingenious etymologies exist. The best definition of cocktail: it's a drink usually chilled by ice, generally combining a spirituous base with one or several flavoring agents.

Cocktail glasses   *See pages 8-10.*

Cointreau   A cognac-based liqueur flavored with peel of bitter Curaçao oranges.

Congeners   Toxic impurities found to some extent in all alcoholic beverages. Several medical studies have implicated the congeners in symptoms such as headaches, gastric irritations, hangover, restless sleep and fatigue. Congener content in alcoholic beverages varies widely. According to some studies, the average bourbon, for example, has more than 200 times more congeners than the average vodka. Congeners is an umbrella term covering several impurities, including methanol, proponal, butanol, acetaldehyde, furfural, esters and tannins. They're present in minute quantities and form as a result of various factors involved in production. Once formed, they cannot be filtered out. They can only be removed by more distillations. Congeners are actually responsible for the hearty, robust flavors of many alcoholic drinks. When drunk in moderation, they will probably cause you no discomfort unless you are among those persons particularly susceptible to their effects. If you want to reduce your intake of congeners, drink gin or vodka.

As an example, here is a short table of the congener content, in milligrams, per standard serving of various brands of beer, wine, and distilled spirits.

Beers

Budweiser	142.5
Michelob	48.6
Michelob Lite	120.1
Miller	64.3

Wines

Taylor Tawny Port	93.7
Martini & Rossi Dry Vermouth	108.4
Gallo Burgundy	62.9
Almaden Rose	77.3

Distilled Spirits

Skyy Vodka	0
Smirnoff Vodka (80 proof)	15.7
J&B Scotch	20.3
Coronet Brandy	36.5
Gordon's Dry Gin	6.8
Bacardi Light Rum	16.8
Hiram Walker Whiskey	11.5
Dewar's Scotch	48.6
Schnapps	12.8
Amaretto Liqueur	13.2

Curaçao Generic name for any liqueur flavored with the peel of bitter Curaçao oranges.

Corks Wine bottle stoppers made from the bark from the cork trees of Portugal.

Crème de This phrase in the name of a liqueur signals that it contains at least 2.5% sugar by volume. Crème liqueurs are mellow, smooth, and sweet.

Crème de Cacao Chocolate-flavored liqueur.

Crème de Cafe Coffee-flavored liqueur (the best known is Mexican Kahlua).

Crème de Cassis Black-currant-flavored liqueur.

Crème de Noyaux Almond-flavored liqueur.

Crème de Menthe Peppermint-flavored liqueur.

Dubonnet A French patent aperitif wine made with aromatic flavorings, slightly quinine-like.

Drambuie Patent brand of honey- and malt whisky-based liqueur.

Fermentation The process in which agents such as yeast, mold, or bacteria split complex organic compounds into relatively simple substances: for example the conversion of sugar to carbon dioxide, or of yeast to alcohol.

Fernet Branca A patent aperitif. Like Lillet and Dubonnet, a flavored and fortified wine.

Fortified wines Wines made strong by the addition of brandy. Even with the most careful cold alcohol fermentation, it's difficult to produce wine with an alcoholic content above 14% since wine yeasts die at that level of alcohol. A jolt of brandy that brings the alcoholic content to around 20% stabilizes the wine, allows it to keep without spoiling. Sherries and ports, vermouths, Madeira, and Marsala are fortified wines.

Frangelico Hazelnut-flavored liqueur.

Galliano A sweet patent liqueur with a complex bouquet of flavorings.

Gin Grain neutral spirits flavored by being distilled or re-distilled with juniper berries and often other aromatics. The name is derived from *genever,* the Dutch word for juniper. Gin, like vodka, is not aged.

Grand Marnier Cognac-based liqueur.

Grappa A fiery spirit distilled from fermented grape pomace, the pulpy residue of the crushing process—skins, seeds, and stems. Called *marc* in France, *aguardiente* in Spain, *tresterschnaps* in Germany.

Grenadine A non-alcoholic red syrup made of sugar and pomegranate juice used to sweeten and color drinks.

Kahlua   Mexican coffee liqueur.

Kirsch   Cherry-flavored liqueur.

Kümmel   Caraway- and anise-flavored liqueur.

Jug wines   Inexpensive table wines (that is, a wine blended from more than one grape and vineyard's production) and bottled in containers of 1.5 and 3 liters.

Lager   *See Beer.* A generic term for all bottom-fermented beers. The term *lagering* means "storing" and bottom-fermented beers are stored, or matured, or lagered, for several months to allow time for a secondary fermentation.

Lillet   A patent aperitif.

Liqueurs   Also called cordials, liqueurs are built on a spirits base, sweetened, and flavored with essences derived from fruits, roots, barks, herbs, flowers, and seeds, each according to a secret recipe. In recipes, liqueurs may be called for generically — in which case you can use any liqueur with the specified flavor, from any maker — or according to formal, proprietary name, or "brand name." Some proprietary patent liqueurs have no generic equivalent, and are based on old, secret recipes with intriguing histories.

Madeira   Fortified wine.

Malt Liquor   Beer with a higher than usual proof. *See Proof. See Beer.*

Maraschino   Liqueur flavored with Yugoslavian cherries.

Marsala   Fortified wine.

Muddling   Bruising an ingredient, such as mint leaves, with a muddling tool or the back of a spoon, to release some of their essence and bouquet into a drink. The word comes from Old Dutch for mixing or jumbling. A bartender's muddler looks something like a miniature baseball bat.

Napa   The valley of the Napa River, about 40 miles northeast of San Francisco, with a marvelous microclimate—warm days, cool nights—ideal from growing wine grapes. In Napa, and in Sonoma to the west, and Lake and Mendocino counties to the north, are made some of the best wines of the United States.

Orange Bitters   *See Bitters.*

Orgeat Syrup   Non-alcoholic almond-flavored sugar syrup used to flavor drinks.

Pernod   Liqueur flavored with anise, fennel, and licorice. A substitute for the now illegal wormwood-flavored absinthe.

Pilsener or Pilsner   *See Beer.* The world's most famous beer style, first brewed at Pilsen, Bohemia, in 1842, where Pilsener Urquell is still produced. Characterized by brightness and dry hoppiness. The classic Pilsener (or Pilsner) glass, is a long conical class resting on a small foot, although commercial establishments use several glass types they refer to as pilsners.

Poire-Williams Pear brandy from Switzerland and France. The most expensive and spectacular of these contains a real, whole pear, grown inside the bottle by tying the bottle onto the branch, over the blossom.

Port Fortified red wine of Oporto, Portugal, quite sweet, esteemed as a dessert wine. Ports are made in California and elsewhere, too, but are generally not as rich or as sweet as the genuine article.

Porter Originally a local London beer made with roasted, unmalted barley, well hopped and blended. Still brewed, but by bottom-fermentation, in many countries.

Pousse-cafe A drink of many colors made by floating liqueurs in layers in a small straight glass. To make a poussé-cafe, one has to know the specific gravity of each constituent layer—brandy, crème de menthe, crème de cacao, and so forth—and possess cool nerve and manual dexterity as well.

Proof Alcoholic content of spirits, the proof number being twice the percentage of alcohol by volume; for example, 100 proof is 50% alcohol, 80 proof is 40%. The alcoholic content of wines is described directly as a percentage by volume, 11%, 12.5%, and so on.

U. S. law forbids beer labels from showing the percentage of alcohol but beer ranges from 3 to 3.5%, ales are generally around 4%, some stouts and malt liquors go as high as 7.5%, though they're usually a good deal less.

Retsina Often referred to as an acquired taste, this is Greek table wine to which pine resin has been added.

Riesling The grape variety from which is produced many of the rich white wines of Alsace, France, and those of the Rheingau, along the Rhine in southwestern Germany. Some excellent ones are also produced in California.

Rose's Lime Juice Sweetened lime-flavored syrup.

Rum Spirits distilled from sugar-cane juice, sugar syrup, or molasses. Rum varies considerably from the very lightest and driest to heavy, dark, sweet. Bacardi, transplanted post-Castro to Puerto Rico, Don Q and Ron Rico, Myers's from Jamaica, and Cruzan from the Virgin Islands, are almost the most popular brands. Proof is usually 80, but a rum of 151 proof is available and may be used to add a certain fiery piquance to such cocktails as Mai Tais and Zombies.

Rye Spirits distilled from a mash of at least 51% rye; the remainder is usually corn and barley. By law, it must be aged for at least one year in new charred oak barrels. Rye is authentic American whiskey, the particular pride of Pennsylvania and Maryland, but is not much in favor these days, Old Overholt (often fondly called Old Overcoat) being virtually the only brand commonly available.

Saké Japanese beverage brewed from rice. Though called "wine," saké is, strictly speaking, a sort of beer because it's made from a grain mash, not from grapes or other fruits, and the yeast used is different from wine yeasts, (and from the usual brewers' yeast) too. (The same is true of a similar beverage, "suk" from Korea.) Traditionally served warm in small porcelain cups.

Sambuca Intensely licorice-flavored liqueur

Sauternes As produced by a few great Bordeaux chateaus, most notably Yquem, it is a sweet dessert wine made at great expense by painstakingly picking over the vineyard as many as eight or nine times to select grapes that have been attacked by "noble rot," *botrytis cinerea*, which removes moisture from them, concentrating their juice. (Made the same way are the great sweet German wines denomi-nated *auslese, beerenauslese, and trockenbeerenauslese.*) Otherwise, sauternes (or sauterne) is a white wine, made in Bordeaux and elsewhere, drunk chilled.

Schnapps Spirits commonly distilled from fruit. *See Aquavit.*

Scotch whisky The distinctive smoky taste of Scotch whisky comes from roasting the malted (sprouted) barley over open peat fires. Single malt or straight Scotch whisky is hearty, flavorful stuff; some respected brands are Glenfiddich, Glenlivet, and Laphroig. Blended Scotch whisky, by far the most popular, is made from a blending of pot-still single-malts lightened with patent-still grain whisky.

Seltzer Unflavored, unsweetened effervescent water.

Sherry Fortified wine of Spain, named after Jerez de la Frontera, blended and aged via the solera: the great barrels are stacked three rows high; wine for bottling is drawn from the lowest row and replen-ished from the second row, which in turn is replenished from the youngest wine from the top row. In good examples, sherry is an elegant wine with a nutty flavor. In de-scending order of dryness: Fino, Amontillado, oloroso, cream (or milk). A chilled fino or Amontillado makes an excellent aperitif.

Sloe The sour, small fruit of the blackthorn, used to flavor the liqueur known as sloe gin.

Sonoma *See Napa.*

Southern Comfort Liqueur Bourbon-based peach-flavored liqueur.

Stills Pot stills are the traditional,

original stills, and consist of a pear-shaped copper boiler into which a batch of fermented mash is introduced. The pot still is heated to a temperature that causes alcohols and some of their congeners to boil off. Alcohol boils, that is, vaporizes, at a lower temperature than water—the secret of distillation. A copper tube in the neck of the pot still carries off the distillate, usually through coils that lose heat either to the surrounding atmosphere or to a jacket of cooling water, so that the distillate is cooled and condensed into alcohol and whatever congeners have emerged with it. The pot still is a batch process; after each charge is heated, the still must be cooled down and cleaned out. Consequently, it is not as efficient as the patent or continuous, columnar still, invented in 1830, into which new mash is introduced onto perforated plates at the top, exhausted mash removed at the bottom.

Stout or Bitter Stout The national beer of Ireland, exemplified by the famous Guinness brew of Dublin, although beers of similar style are brewed in various parts of the world.

Strega Spicy yellow liqueur.

Sulfites Wine, as a complex, living, natural product, despite careful fining and filtration, is bound to contain many living microscopic creatures, fungi and bacteria,

mostly, that will affect wine in unwanted ways. (At the very least, they will cause an unsightly sediment to form at the bottom of the bottle.) Sulphur compounds have been used for hundreds of years to kill these growths; recently, U.S. law has required wine makes to reveal on the label that they've used sulphur compounds to clarify and stabilize their product.

Superfine sugar Very finely processed sugar, used in drink-making because it dissolves quickly.

Tennessee Sour Mash A straight whiskey made in Tennessee from a mash containing at least 51% of a single grain, generally corn, started with mash from a previous run, and filtered through charcoal. George Dickel and Jack Daniel's are the sole makers.

Tequila Spirits distilled from *pulque*, the fermented mash of the mezcal, known also as the century or agave plant, a type of aloe, not a cactus.

Tia Maria Coffee liqueur from Jamaica.

Tonic Water Sweetened and lightly flavored carbonated water containing quinine.

Triple Sec White curaçao. *See Curaçao.*

Vandermint Chocolate-mint flavored liqueur.

Varietal Wines Wines labeled by the grape variety they contain.

Examples are: pinot noir, cabernet sauvignon, merlot, chenin blanc, sylvaner, traminer, riesling, gamay, chardonnary, zinfandel. Sometimes, 100% of a particular variety is necessary to qualify, but usually some lesser but predominating percentage is allowed by law. In the U.S., the use of names like Champagne, Burgundy, Rhine Wine, Chablis, and so on, does not mean that these wines are made from particular grapes, but only that they're considered to resemble in style the European originals.

Vermouth A fortified aperitif wine flavored with as many as thirty or forty different herbs, flowers, roots, berries, or seeds. Served chilled as an appetizer. Dry white vermouth is a necessary component of a Martini, sweet red, of a Manhattan.

Vintage The year a wine was made; the wine made that year.

Vodka Neutral spirits, almost always derived from a grain mash. The goal of the vodka maker is a clear, colorless, pure spirit, free of adulterants and congeners. To achieve this goal, a grain mash is carefully distilled, rectified (re-distilled to reduce adulterants), filtered through charcoal.

Weisse Bier Classical, refreshing wheat beer originating in Germany.

Whiskey Spirits distilled from a grain mash. (Scots and Canadians spell it whisky.) The word derives, so the etymologists say, from *uisquebeatha*, "water of life" in Gaelic, and so is a cognate of eau-de-vie, which means the same in French, and to vodka, the Slavic ironic-diminutive-affectionate—"dear little water."

INDEX